P9-CKU-148

027.073
D561

THE LIBRARY IN AMERICA

A Celebration in Words and Pictures

by

PAUL DICKSON

WITHDRAWN

Facts On File Publications
New York, New York • Oxford, England

LIBRARY ST. MARY'S COLLEGE
166425

The Library in America:
A Celebration in Words and Pictures

Copyright © 1986 Paul Dickson

All rights reserved.
No part of this book may be reproduced
or utilized in any form or by any means,
electronic or mechanical, including photocopying,
recording or by any information storage and retrieval systems,
without permission in writing from the Publisher.

Library of Congress Cataloging-in-Publication Data

Dickson, Paul.
   The library in America.

   Bibliography: p.
   Includes index.
   1. Libraries—United States.   I. Title.
Z731.D48 1986   027.073   86-8981
ISBN 0-8160-1365-9

Designed by *Oksana Kushnir*

The Author here wishes to thank the following parties for permission to reprint copyrighted materials (selections are listed in order of appearance in the book):

"A Ventriloquist Comes to Boston," Copyright © 1949, by the Graduate Library School, University of Chicago.

"October 4, 1876, Philadelphia," Copyright © 1976, by John Bergamini. Reprinted by permission of McIntosh and Otis, Inc.

"Little Room for Children" and "Special Collections: A Case in Point," Copyright © 1972 by C. H. Cramer. Reprinted from *Open Shelves and Open Minds.*

"Father Andy's Social Ideas," reprinted by permission of the American Library Association, from *Arsenals of a Democratic Culture*, by Sidney Ditzion, Copyright © 1947 by the American Library Association.

"The Woman Library Worker," reprinted with permission of the Free Press, a Division of Macmillan, Inc., from *Apostles of Culture: A Study of the American Public Library 1876–1920*, by Dee Garrison, Copyright © 1979 by the Free Press.

"Lenin on the 'Profane Use of Librarianship,'" from *Lenin, Krupskaia and Libraries*, Copyright © 1968. Used by permission of the Shoe String Press, Inc.

"When Libraries Take to the Open Road," and "The Dewey–Casanova Syndrome," Copyright © 1926/1976 by the New York Times Company. Reprinted by permission.

"How a Black Man Got Books from the Memphis Library," pp. 268–71, in *Black Boy: A Record of Childhood and Youth*, by Richard Wright. Copyright © 1937, 1942, 1944, 1945 by Richard Wright. Reprinted by permission of Harper & Row, Publishers, Incorporated.

"The WPA Comes to Minneapolis," from the section by John Franklin White, in *Studies in Creative Partnership*, edited by Daniel F. Ring. Copyright © 1980 by Daniel F. Ring. Reprinted with the permission of the Author and Scarecrow Press, Inc.

"A Week in the Life of a Book Bus, Hibbing, Minnesota," reprinted from *Library Journal*, September 1, 1930. Published by R. R. Bowker Co. Copyright © 1930 by R. R. Bowker Co.

"A Romance for Classifiers Only," reprinted by permission from the *Wilson Library Bulletin.*

"Facing Armageddon," from *Forbidden Books in American Public Libraries, 1876–1939*, by Evelyn Geller. Copyright © 1984 by Evelyn Geller. Reprinted by permission of Greenwood Press, a division of Congressional Information Services, Inc.

"A European Librarian Looks at the Big City Library," reprinted by permission of the American Library Association, from *American Librarianship from a European Angle*, by William Munthe. Copyright © 1939 by the American Library Association.

"From *The Diary of a Village Library*," by Caroline M. Lord, New Hampshire Publishing Co., Somersworth, NH, 1971.

"The Librarian and the Democratic Process," reprinted by permission of the American Library Association, from *Champion of a Cause*, by Archibald MacLeish. Copyright © 1971 by the American Library Association.

"On the Front with Wodehouse and Waugh," reprinted by permission of the American Library Association, from an article by William Cole in the April 1976 *American Libraries*. Copyright © 1976 by the American Library Association.

"The Molesworth Institute," reprinted by permission of Norman D. Stevens and the American Library Association, from *The ALA Bulletin*. Copyright © 1963 by the American Library Association.

"Urban Libraries" and "The Universal Library Card." Copyright © The Washington Post. Reprinted by permission.

"Anybody Got Fifteen Cents?" from *Tales of Melvil's Mouser or Much Ado About Libraries*, by Paul Dunkin, published by R. R. Bowker, Division of Reed Publishing, USA. Copyright © 1970 by Reed Publishing USA, a Division of Reed Holdings, Inc. All rights reserved.

"When Readers Become Suspects," Copyright © 1970 Southern Regional Council.

"Library Verse," Copyright © 1986, Pyke Johnson, Jr.

"Fire Reminiscent of the Dark Ages," by Jack Smith. Copyright © 1982, Los Angeles Times, reprinted by permission.

"The Library of the Future," Copyright © 1985, *The Futurist*, The World Future Society, Bethesda, MD.

Film still reproduced on page 223 from *Ghostbusters*. Courtesy of Columbia Pictures.

Printed in the United States of America

10 9 8 7 6 5 4 3 2 1

Dedicated
to the professionals and volunteers
who made all of this possible
with a special nod to those workaday librarians
who are always helping us,
but who we seldom take time to thank

Mural Inscription at the Chicago Public Library Cultural Center

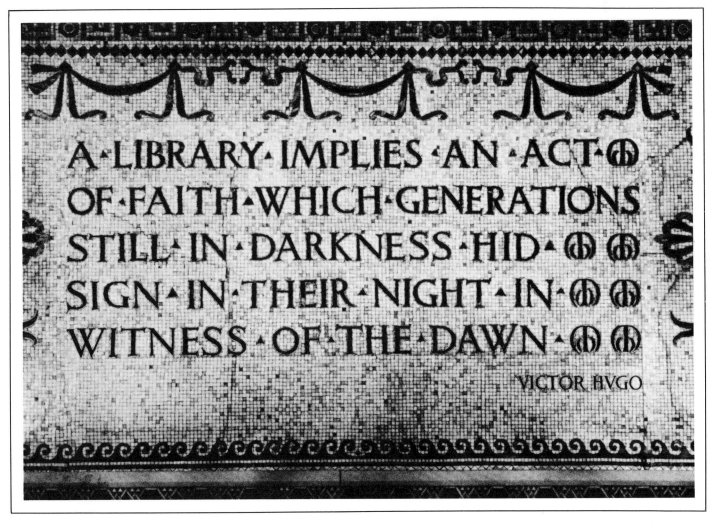

CONTENTS

ACKNOWLEDGMENTS

A number of people have helped in the preparation of this book. I would like to thank them:

Anthony Arms, Dauphin Public Library System; Rick J. Ashton, Denver Public Library; Susan Avallone, *Library Journal*; R. S. Balister, Charlottesville, Virginia; Peggy Barber, American Library Association; Karla Innis Barde; Toni Carbo Bearman, National Commission on Libraries and Information Science; Sanford Berman, Hennepin County Library; John Berry, *Library Journal*; Blaise Bisaillon, Forbes Library, Northampton, Massachusetts; Charles Blank, Washington County Free Library; Rich Bowra, Dauphin County Library System; Anne F. Briggs, Kent County Library; Muriel Breitenbach, ALA; Lynda W. Brown, George Mason University; Nancy Bush, Library of Congress; John Y. Cole, Center for the Book, Library of Congress; Evelyn Cooperman, San Diego Public Library; Mary Corliss, Museum of Modern Art Film Still Archives; Dan Crawford; William Rossa Cole, New York City; Susan Cummings, Maryland State Archives; Nancy Debevoise, Washington, D.C.; Nancy DeLury, Pikes Peak Library District; Don Ellinghausen, ALA Archives; Joan Erwin, Orange County Library System; Gordon Flagg, *American Libraries*; Robert D. Franklin, Charlottesville; Roy M. Fry, Office of Education; Robert Garen, Detroit Public Library; Robert Gaylor, Oakland University; Terry Geiskin, Museum of Modern Art Film Still Archives; Kristi Gibson, Minneapolis Public Library; Joseph C. Goulden, Washington, D.C.; Dorothy P. Gray, National Commission on Libraries and Information Sciences; Agnes Griffin, Montgomery County Public Libraries; Linda Griffin, San Diego Public Library; Carol Habinski, Findlay Hancock Public Library; Colin B. Hamer, Jr., New Orleans Public Library; John W. Hammond, Kansas City Public Library; Patricia Haynes, Carnegie Corporation of New York; Elizabeth C. Hoke, Montgomery County Public Libraries; Lloyd T. Hooker, Federal Prison System Librarian; Peggy Hull, Durham, North Carolina; Marilyn M. Jacobs, National Agricultural Library; Warren R. Johnston, Woolwich, Maine; Averil J. Kadis, Enoch Pratt Free Library; Bernard S. Katz, Reston, Virginia; Annette Curtis Klause, Montgomery Public Libraries; Laura Linard, Chicago Public Library; Jane Lowenthal, Carnegie Endowment; Ann M. Loyd, Carnegie Library of Pittsburgh; Sarah McGarry, Phoenix Public Library; Susan Malus, Brooklyn Public Library; Risto Marttinen; Grace K. Maxfield, Ann Arbor, Michigan; Roy Meador, Ann Arbor; Carol McCabe, Juneau Public Library; Thomas P. McNally, Free Library of Philadelphia; Mary Miklasz, St. Louis Public Library; Arthur Milner, Free Library of Philadelphia; Barbara Moro, Chicago Public Library; Susan Mower, Albert S. Cook Library; Kent Mulliner, Assistant to Director of Libraries, Ohio University Libraries; Ann Olszewski, Cleveland Public Library; Denys Parsons; Herbert Paper, Hebrew Union College; Louis Phillips, New York City; Art Plotnik, *American Libraries*; Diane Rafferty, National Commission on Libraries and Information Science; Michele Raphoon, Cooper–Hewitt Museum; Robert G. Reagan, Los Angeles Public Library; Julia L. Reed, Waupaca Library System; B. B. Rile, Wabash College Library; Robert W. Roehr, St. Louis Public Library; Amy Ryan, Minneapolis Public Library; Samuel Sass, Pittsfield, Massachusetts; Sonja J. Scarseth, Aurora University Library; Janie Schomberg, Edgerton School, Roseville, Minnesota; Michele Schuster, Montgomery County Libraries; Herbert W. Sewell, Madison, Wisconsin; Norman J. Shaffer, Library of Congress; Janet A. Shinheit, Librarian, Nelson Wheeler Library, Worcester, Massachusetts; Paul C. Spehr, Library of Congress; Lee Ann Sperling, Rochester Public Library; Norman D. Stevens, Storrs, Connecticut; John Sullivan, Library of Congress; Peggy Thomson, Washington, D.C.; James Thorpe III, Shoestring Press; C. J. Trimble, Denver Public Library; Bobbie Waybright, Enoch Pratt Free Library; Chris Wagner, Madison, Wisconsin; Daniela Weiss, New York Public Library; Marvin Y. Whiting, Birmingham Public Library; Carol W. Wilkinson, West Virginia University Libraries, Margaret L. Young, Gale Research.

There are numerous men and women perambulating the earth—
in appearance much like ordinary respectable citizens—who have warm,
loving, passionate—even sensuous—feelings about libraries....

—Elinor Lander Horwitz, writing in *The Washington Star*,
November 15, 1970

The affliction lacks a proper name, but a lot of us have it and most of us are not looking for a cure. It is the passion for libraries.

Mine began to stir in the 1940s at the old Carnegie Public Library in Yonkers, New York, which to this kid was the most important and impressive place in town. It sat on the side of a hill and had an odd, elliptical shape to accommodate its position. A quirky set of offset, hillside steps got you into the place, which always seemed at its most inviting on the coldest and hottest days. It was as if it was warmed in the winter by its shell of bright yellow brick—it looked like a lemon Beaux Arts birthday cake—and cooled in the summer by the tons of white marble that covered the inside. The grand staircase led up to a juvenile department that seemed to catch a particular slant of sunlight from the oversized second-story windows. The lightfall moved across the room as the afternoon wore on, and you could get a pretty good idea of what time it was getting to be by looking down at the floor.

Later I took my business downstairs to the Young Adult Room, where there were no story hours or puppet shows and where the books all seemed to have dark bindings, ranging in tone from plum to prune. One day when I couldn't find what I wanted in "YA," which was how all the books there were marked, I was sent to the reference room, where it seemed that all the information in the world must be stored. It was here, for example, that I became fascinated with facts such as that even dentists and librarians had patron saints (St. Apollonia and St. Jerome, respectively) and that the first recorded unassisted triple play in baseball was made by Paul Hines in 1878.

INTRODUCTION

The Carnegie Library in Yonkers. As it appeared in a postcard of the 1940s. (Author's collection)

YONKERS PUBLIC LIBRARY. SOUTH BROADWAY. YONKERS. N. Y.

Despite a late attempt by local preservationists to save it, the wrecking ball took the place away about four years ago so the street could be widened. In 1980 the library had moved into a refurbished department store a few blocks away and lives on in spirit if not in the same style.

I mourn the loss of the old building for a strictly personal reason: I'd like to be able to go back there from time to time and catch the light in the children's room or dwell in the reference room long enough to find a book that told me *how* Paul Hines got his one-man triple play. (This is small consolation, but it was the library used in the library scenes in the 1969 film *Goodbye Columbus*, so I can still get to see it once in a blue moon—see page 181.)

But it is gone, and I can thank it for giving me that passion for books and libraries, which is now in an advanced stage.

My symptoms are not atypical. I am fascinated by the romance, lore, and culture of American libraries. I am a self-confessed library buff, drawn to them like others are drawn to theaters, art galleries, bars, or football games. I am proud to say that I have more library cards than credit cards in my wallet and that I know where all the coffee machines are located at the Library of Congress. I think a run to the library can salvage an otherwise blah day, and I was shocked recently when a well-known writer on the subject of personal computers opened his syndicated column by saying that he was looking for a data base that would save him "trips to the library."

If I have two hours to kill in a strange city I will prowl the local library looking for that which sets it apart, whether it be the fantastic automotive collection at the Detroit Public Library, the collection of early English humor at the main Cincinnati Library, the H. L. Mencken room at the Enoch Pratt Library in Baltimore, or the Western Americana collection at the library in Fryeburg, Maine (this last being the gift of Clarence Mumford, creator of Hopalong Cassidy, who spent most of his life in Fryeburg).

I have fallen in love with several libraries. The special library at the Baseball Hall of Fame in Cooperstown, N.Y., is one. I once got to spend a blissful three days there "working" on a project. Another is a collection at the San Francisco Public Library called the Schmulowitz Collection of Wit and Humor (SCOWAH). It is the world's largest collection of humor, containing 17,000 books and many magazines. To the humor lover, it is the Louvre and Sistine Chapel rolled into one. The late Nate Schmulowitz, a lawyer, put the collection together to rectify the fact that few major libraries ever really collected humor.

I have visited a library in Clearwater, Florida, that was so small that it could not be called a branch but a twig. The Clearwater East Twig Library recently closed, to be replaced by a proper branch, but I will cherish the memory of that glorified broom closet and its charming name.

I am totally infatuated with the small country libraries that are still vital community centers and points of local pride, despite shoestring budgets. While traveling, I will invent the most preposterous excuses—"Oh my gosh! I've forgotten the name of Warren Harding's vice president, and it's driving me nuts"—to justify stopping in a small-town library to drink in its special atmosphere and predilections.

One of my favorites is in the small town of Weld, Maine—a handsome, professionally run, free, public library supported solely by its population of 320 people. It is open only three days a week and, yes, it has *Megatrends* among its collection of nearly 10,000 books.

The reason for this book is that I had been looking for a way to celebrate this fascination and translate it into something tangible. I began looking after reading an article in the *New York Times* on the failing campaign to save *my* old library in Yonkers from the road wideners.

I wanted to do something that would dramatize the fact that America has created the best collection of public libraries in the world. They can hardly be called a system since their individual policies, plans, and close to 80 percent of their funding comes from local sources; yet they work better than most systems. I wanted to show that a lot had gone into the American library movement. I felt that perhaps too many people were taking it all for granted—amid all the fund raisers, bond campaigns, and fights for longer hours and book collections. One day at my local library I listened to a patron complain bitterly about the fact that a mystery novel that had been reviewed in the *Washington Post* had not yet been ordered. The patron stormed off after promising to write an angry letter to the librarian in charge of the county system. All I could think of was that this person, as many of us do from time to time, had lost all perspective on the public library and the struggle that had gone into creating it. Lest we forget, there is nothing in the Constitution that guarantees us a book on Monday just because it was reviewed in the paper on Sunday.

Along with this lack of perspective, I have been amazed that much of what one gets to read about libraries these days seems to be about the technical aspects of library automation, the agonizing death of the card catalog, fines policies, book thieves, budgetary constraints, or the pressures to ban some book that is offensive to some group. These are all important things but are hardly uplifting, reflective themes.

My plan went through several incarnations, but what finally occurred to me was to reflect on the story of the American public library through pictures—good, solid photographs mixed in with what I will call verbal snapshots. It was not to be an attempt at an all-inclusive history of the library movement but rather a scrapbook of that movement, using imagery that is old but I hope fresh, in that most of it has not been seen anywhere for decades. This notion was made most graphic when my eyes first glimpsed a pack of Works Progress Administration photographs at the National Archives. They were taken in the late 1930s and showed librarians on the backs of horses and mules hauling books up into the hollows of Tennessee. For me, these pictures summoned up the idealism of the time in a way that no government report on the WPA could accomplish.

It is through such pictures that this book is meant to be a valentine to libraries, librarians, and patrons smitten with a passion for libraries.

After some months of photo research, it would appear that American library life has been well-documented, and is being well preserved at such places as the American Library Association Archives at the University of Illinois, the ALA itself, the National Archives, and the Library of Congress. The same can be said for individual libraries, both large and small, some of whose fine collections are credited throughout the book.

For all of this, however, there are some big blunders being committed by libraries. It would not do to name names in a valentine, but the public relations director for one large urban system told me that all the event and publicity photographs having to do with the library before 1980 had been disposed of—I was too cowardly to ask how—because they were taking up too much room. I was told by a librarian who had recently gotten rid of several file folders of photographs that I would not have been interested in them anyway because they were "old and obsolete." An administrator for another large system told me on the morning we had an appointment to see her institution's picture collection that she had just been informed that the collection was "off limits" to the public.

I hope that the pictures used in this book reflect well on the photographers who took them, on the subjects themselves, and on the people who have preserved them. If nothing else, I hope it has a visual impact that will prevent any other institution from tossing out images just to make room in the files. I would also like to make the modest proposal that at some time soon an effort should be launched to make sure that elements of this visual history not be pitched and at least be offered to the ALA Archives rather than the nearest dumpster.

PAUL DICKSON

Garrett Park, Maryland
Spring 1986

BEGINNINGS OF THE MOVEMENT

The first library in America was founded in 1638 at Harvard University. A few churches also established small parish libraries in the colonial period, but these had little effect on the average man.

As did so many other things in America, libraries got their start with the help of Benjamin Franklin. Finding that books were expensive and hard to get hold of in colonial Philadelphia, Franklin hit on the idea of pooling the resources of a number of young men, who banded together in 1731 to start a subscription library, the Philadelphia Library Company. The pattern established by that group was followed again and again. These social libraries were not public libraries but rather their forerunners.

ONE

Ephemera Established by 140 well-to-do New Yorkers, the Society Library was founded in 1754. It was an important early subscription library which, according to a newspaper ad from 1763, featured "several Thousand Volumes of Choice Books, in History, Divinity, Travels, Voyages, Novels, &c." Shown here are (*right*) a receipt given to a member for 1796 and an important NOTICE. (The Smithsonian)

New-York, 1796

Mr. James M. Hughes

To the New-York Society Library, Dr.

To your annual Subscription for 2 Shares due 3 May, 1795 £1 0 0

To Do — Do — 3 — 1796 1 0 0

To fines 2 1 11

Received Payment, £4 1 11

NOTICE.

The Trustees of the New-York Society Library deem it their duty to request all persons interested in the institution to exercise a little care in preventing the Books from getting injured when taken out of the Library. They are frequently blotted, scribbled in, and torn by children, and often soiled by servants bringing them to the Library without an envelope.

It should also be remembered, that no person has a right to insert any comments, however correct, in the margin, or other parts of a Book, either with a pen or pencil. This practice induces others to disfigure the page with idle and unnecessary remarks.

According to the By Laws of the Society, any person losing or injuring a Book is liable to make reparation to the full value of the whole set to which the volume may belong.

THE IMPACT OF FRANKLIN'S LIBRARY 1731

The year 1731 began a new era in the intellectual life of the American people, an era of co-operation for the procurement of books. It was in that year that Benjamin Franklin, because he was a lover of books and because books were so rare and expensive that they could only be obtained with great difficulty, proposed to the Junto, a half-social, half-literary society, of which he was a member, that they bring their books to the club, where they might be enjoyed by all. The result was the formation of the Philadelphia Library Company—"the mother of all North American subscription libraries."

The foundation of this library was the beginning of an epoch in the library history, not only of this country, but of the world. It was not until twenty-five years later that the first subscription library was established in England—that of Liverpool, in 1756; so that the position which America holds today at the head of all matters pertaining to library advancement and usefulness is a trust direct from the liberty-loving founders of the Republic. It is perhaps significant that this movement for the free use of books owes its origin to the so-called middle class, to the manual laborer rather than the professional man, for Franklin and his friends who subscribed to the stock of the company were mechanics and tradesmen. The library was created, not for the use of the scholar, or the rich, or any one class, but for those people who could not win their way to books through the medium of position or money. Franklin's very simple but hitherto un-thought-of device was a new and radical departure. Its effect was toward a more even distribution of intellectual wealth, the establishment, so to speak, of an intellectual democracy.

Franklin's idea, that of the joint stock library association, was contagious. Naturally adopted first in and about Philadelphia, its territory was soon limited only by the frontiers of the country. Before the first shot of the Revolution was fired at Lexington, the seed of library co-operation had taken firm root and pushed its way through the soil of bookish exclusiveness. The library of the Carpenter's Company, Philadelphia, was founded in 1735; Proprietor's library, Pomfret, Conn., 1737; library of the Four Monthly Meetings of Friends, Philadelphia, 1742; Redwood Library, Newport, R.I., 1747: Charleston (S.C.) Library Society, 1748; the curious revolving library which travelled between the first and second parishes in Kittery and York, Me., 1751; Providence Library, united in 1856 with the Providence Athenaeum, 1753; New York Society library, now numbering more than ninety thousand volumes, 1754; Union library, Hatborough, Penn., 1755; library of the Winyaw Indigo Society of Georgetown, S.C., 1755; New England library, Boston, 1758; Prince library, Boston, 1758; Social library, Salem, Mass., 1760; Social library, Leominster, Mass., 1763; Portland library, 1763; Chester (Pa.) library, 1769; and Social library, Hingham, Mass., 1773.

These libraries represent the chief means of general literary culture open to Americans prior to the Revolutionary War. The idea of the Free public library as it is understood today had not been conceived; but in that third step of library progress, co-operation, the craving for books, opened a new avenue of accessibility, the avenue which was destined in the course of time to broaden into the toil-less highway of practically unrestricted procurement.

—From "The Public Library in the United States," by Joseph Leroy Harrison, which appeared in *The New England Magazine*, August 1894.

Book Burners In August 1814 the British set fire to the U.S. Capitol, destroying among other things the Congressional library. A few days later, ex-President Thomas Jefferson offered to sell his fine library as a replacement. It contained nearly 7,000 volumes and was appraised by Congress at $23,950. Congress appropriated the money but not without some objection. Representative Daniel Webster, among others, voted "Nay." Shown here are *(right)* books from the original Jefferson collection that are still in the Library of Congress and an artist's conception of the burning of the original collection, which uses some artistic license to suggest that the books were actually used to fuel the burning of Congressional furnishings. (Library of Congress)

Boston Public *(Top)* It opened in 1854 as the first urban public library in America with goals that included the preservation of the community. Modern scholars term it the institution that began the modern library movement in America. (From *Ballou's*)

First The first public library in America came into being in Peterboro, New Hampshire, in 1833 and holds claim to the title of being the oldest free library in the world supported by taxation. The building shown here *(right)* was erected in 1892. (Author's collection)

The Athenaeum Founded in 1807 in Boston, the Athenaeum was a variation on the social library, catering to the city's most influential citizens. Athenaeums in Boston and New York inspired the foundation of similar institutions in smaller cities. Shown *(left)* are an exterior and an interior view of the Boston Athenaeum in the building whose cornerstone was laid in 1847. (From *Ballou's Pictorial Drawing-Room Companion*)

Pay as You Go This receipt from the Library Company of Philadelphia, deemed by Franklin himself as the "Mother of all the North American subscription libraries," brings home the reality that such places were not for those who could not afford them. Inflation had begun to set in by 1815, because the original fee for belonging was 40 shillings for a share of stock and ten shillings a year to support the book fund. (The Smithsonian)

Conditions The Boston Circulating Library was typical of the early libraries that operated in conjunction with a private business. The proprietor also sold "fancy goods," stationery, and music. The list of conditions shown here underscores the business side of such libraries. (Smithsonian)

No. 7 **Library Company of Philadelphia.**

RECEIVED, the *first* day of May, Anno Domini 18 *15* of *Anthony Morris* fifteen shillings in full of the Payment on the share held in that name for the last year, and twenty shillings, the amount of the fines incurred for neglecting to make the said Payment agreeably to the Charter and Laws of the Library Company of Philadelphia: also, fifteen shillings in full of the payment for this year.

£ 2 : 10

James P. Parke, Treasurer.

CONDITIONS
OF THE
BOSTON UNION CIRCULATING-LIBRARY,
No. 12, CORNHILL, BOSTON.

ARTICLE 1. *Persons who become subscribers pay in advance on commencing or renewing subscription :*

For a year	7 dollars.
For a half-year	4 dollars.
For a Quarter	2.50 cts.
For a month	1 dollar.

And are entitled to have from the Library four duodecimo, or two octavo volumes at a time---but not to change them oftener than once a day---nor detain any book longer than a month at a time.

ART. 2. *Subscribers lending the books to forfeit their subscriptions ; and all books out beyond the number they are entitled to, will be charged over as non-subscribers.*

ART. 3. NON-SUBSCRIBERS *pay for the books, as returned ; for each duodecimo, or smaller volume, per week, 6¼ cents, and after the third week, 12½ cents ;---For each octavo, 12½ cents, and after the fourth week, 25 cents per week, to the time of its being returned.*

ART. 4. *All books returned, that have been out one day over a week, will be charged as if detained two weeks, and if out one day over two weeks, will be charged as three weeks, and so on.*

ART. 5. *Books not returned within six weeks are considered as purchased, and payment will be exacted for the value of the books to the Librarian, with the remaining volumes of the sets to which they may belong, together with the amount due for detention for all the time the volumes are out, until notice is given at the Library, and payment made agreeably to the 3d Article.*

ART. 6. *The value of the books taken, to be deposited, when required, and all books lost or injured to be paid for agreeably to the 5th Article.* *** *This article applies equally to Subscribers and Non-Subscribers.*

NOTE. *In order that the customers of the Library may be supplied with every work which is scarce and valuable, and in consequence of the high price of English books, the Librarian is frequently obliged to pay an extravagant price for some which are not re-printed in this country : in such cases, he feels himself at liberty to vary the charge for reading, from the above* CONDITIONS *; according, in some measure, to the cost of the volume.*

ADAMS, JEFFERSON, MADISON AND THE LIBRARY OF CONGRESS 1800 TO 1815

President John Adams (1797–1801), for whom the Library's Adams Building is named, approved the Library's founding legislation on April 24, 1800. Five thousand dollars was appropriated to purchase books "for the use of Congress" after it moved from Philadelphia to the new capital city of Washington. The first Library of Congress was a large, centrally located room in the Capitol. Today a plaque near [former] Senate Majority Leader Howard Baker's office marks the approximate location.

Thomas Jefferson is so important to the Library that a principal building has been named for him—twice! The former Annex, now the Adams Building, was the Jefferson Building from 1976 until 1980, when, most appropriately, the Main Building was named for the third President. Bibliophile and book collector extraordinaire, President Thomas Jefferson (1801–1809) approved the 1802 act that provided for the appointment of the Librarian of Congress by the President and gave Congress the power to establish the Library's rules and regulations. The new law also entitled the President and Vice President (and thus the executive branch of government) to use Congress' library. Throughout his presidency, Jefferson personally recommended books for the Library. He also appointed the first two Librarians of Congress, John J. Beckley (1802–1807) and Patrick Magruder (1807–1815). Each received $2 a day for duties performed as Librarian, and also served as Clerk of the House of Representatives.

Jefferson's most important influence on the Library of Congress, however, came after he left the Presidency. In 1815, after the British had destroyed the U.S. Capitol, ex-President Jefferson sold his 6,487-volume library to the Government to "recommence" the Congressional library, forever expanding its scope and ambitions beyond those of a legislative library. Jefferson's rationale, "there is . . . no subject to which a member of Congress may not have occasion to refer" is the rationale for the national and international roles of today's Library of Congress.

The act of Congress authorizing the purchase of Jefferson's library was approved by Jefferson's friend, President James Madison (1809–1817), for whom the Library's largest and most recent building is named. In 1783, as a young member of the Continental Congress, Madison sponsored a proposal for a library for Congress and even drew up a list of over 300 desired books. A bibliophile and perhaps the most intellectual American President, Madison was a philosopher–statesman whose commitment to joining learning and liberty and thus advancing both is chiseled, appropriately enough, on the front of the Madison Building: "What spectacle can be more edifying or more seasonable, than that of Liberty & Learning, each leaning on the other for their mutual and surest support?"

—From the article "The Library of Congress and the Presidential Parade, 1800–1984," by John Y. Cole, from the *Information Bulletin* of the Library of Congress, October 15, 1984.

Calling In an effort to organize the advocates of public libraries, Charles C. Jewett of the Smithsonian called this meeting *(below)* in 1853. Jewett had hoped to set up an association of libraries, a great national library that would operate in conjunction with the Smithsonian and suggested the idea of a unified catalog to list all the books in the nation's libraries. Because of the financial panic of 1857 and the onset of the Civil War the great plans made at this meeting never materialized. One of those institutions that supported the convention was the Massachusetts State Library, which, as shown here, typified the grand and imposing new libraries of the period. (American Library Association and *Ballou's*)

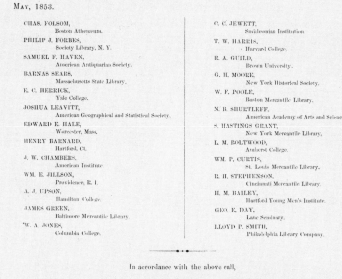

CALL FOR A CONVENTION OF LIBRARIANS.

THE undersigned, believing that the knowledge of Books, and the foundation and management of collections of them for public use, may be promoted by consultation and concert among librarians and others interested in bibliography, respectfully invite such persons to meet

IN CONVENTION AT NEW YORK,

ON THURSDAY, THE FIFTEENTH DAY OF SEPTEMBER,

for the purpose of conferring together upon the means of advancing the prosperity and usefulness of public libraries, and for the suggestion and discussion of topics of importance to book collectors and readers.

MAY, 1853.

CHAS. FOLSOM,
    Boston Athenæum.
PHILIP J. FORBES,
    Society Library, N. Y.
SAMUEL F. HAVEN,
    American Antiquarian Society.
BARNAS SEARS,
    Massachusetts State Library.
E. C. HERRICK,
    Yale College.
JOSHUA LEAVITT,
    American Geographical and Statistical Society.
EDWARD E. HALE,
    Worcester, Mass.
HENRY BARNARD,
    Hartford, Ct.
J. W. CHAMBERS,
    American Institute
WM. E. JILLSON,
    Providence, R. I.
A. J. UPSON,
    Hamilton College.
JAMES GREEN,
    Baltimore Mercantile Library.
W. A. JONES,
    Columbia College.

C. C. JEWETT,
    Smithsonian Institution.
T. W. HARRIS,
    Harvard College.
R. A. GUILD,
    Brown University.
G. H. MOORE,
    New York Historical Society.
W. F. POOLE,
    Boston Mercantile Library.
N. B. SHURTLEFF,
    American Academy of Arts and Sciences.
S. HASTINGS GRANT,
    New York Mercantile Library.
L. M. BOLTWOOD,
    Amherst College.
WM. P. CURTIS,
    St. Louis Mercantile Library.
R. H. STEPHENSON,
    Cincinnati Mercantile Library.
H. M. BAILEY,
    Hartford Young Men's Institute.
GEO. E. DAY,
    Lane Seminary.
LLOYD P. SMITH,
    Philadelphia Library Company.

In accordance with the above call,

THE SMALLER CHAPEL OF THE UNIVERSITY OF THE CITY OF NEW YORK,

SITUATED IN UNIVERSITY PLACE, FRONTING ON WASHINGTON SQUARE,

will be opened for the sessions of the convention on Thursday, September 15th, at 10 o'clock, A. M. Librarians and others, intending to be present at the Convention, are invited, as they come in town, to register their names at the Bookstore of Mr. C. B. NORTON, 71 Chambers Street. Information concerning Libraries not represented, and any letters for the Convention may also be addressed to his care.

NEW YORK, SEPT. 5, 1853.

APPRENTICES' LIBRARY.

Every Book must be returned to the Library, or renewed, within two weeks   The fine for keeping beyond that period.

WILL BE THREE CENTS PER WEEK.

For returning a book with leaves turned down, one cent.

For Scribbling, or any other injury done to the book, fines are to be fixed by the Committee of Attendance.

。 Boys are requested to learn the number on the Card.

BOSTON
Circulating Library Co.,
213 High Street.

CALL AT OUR STORE

And take a book from our Circulating Library by your Favorite Author. We require no deposit.

GRANT & BROWN,
873 Washington St.,
BOSTON.

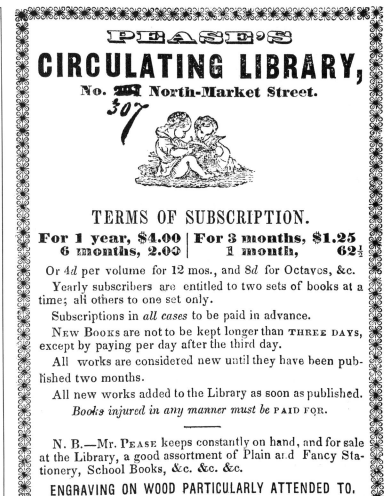

PEASE'S
CIRCULATING LIBRARY,

No. 307 North-Market Street.

TERMS OF SUBSCRIPTION.

For 1 year, $4.00 | For 3 months, $1.25
6 months, 2.00 | 1 month, 62½

Or 4*d* per volume for 12 mos., and 8*d* for Octavos, &c.

Yearly subscribers are entitled to two sets of books at a time; all others to one set only.

Subscriptions in *all cases* to be paid in advance.

NEW BOOKS are not to be kept longer than THREE DAYS, except by paying per day after the third day.

All works are considered new until they have been published two months.

All new works added to the Library as soon as published.

Books injured in any manner must be PAID FOR.

N. B.—Mr. PEASE keeps constantly on hand, and for sale at the Library, a good assortment of Plain and Fancy Stationery, School Books, &c. &c. &c.

ENGRAVING ON WOOD PARTICULARLY ATTENDED TO.

Trade Cards and Broadsides As the new idea of public libraries took hold, it was easy to forget the odd collection of other types of libraries that had served readers for so long. Displayed here are surviving reminders of these places preserved by the Smithsonian. Shown are trade cards *(opposite, bottom; above)* from two of the many commercial circulating libraries that flourished in Boston from 1765 through the 1860s, an advertisement for a similar institution in Philadelphia *(above, right)* and a book plate from an apprentices' library *(opposite, top).* Apprentices' and mechanics' libraries served young artisans and were often supported by their employers. They were to be found in major cities from San Francisco to Portland, Maine. (The Smithsonian)

A VENTRILOQUIST COMES TO BOSTON 1841

Socially, Boston of the 1840's was ripe for a public library. The community had survived the vicissitudes of political controversy and a second war with England. It had regained its economic stability and once again could look upon the future with confidence. A new wealth was being created by men of such commercial eminence as Joshua Bates and George Peabody, who maintained offices in London and were important in the life of the Massachusetts capital. Though Emerson might suffer fears that the swiftly increasing power of wealth would "upset the balance of man, and establish a new universal monarchy more tyrannical than Babylon or Rome," class cleavages were not yet sharply drawn. Boston, like other cities of the period, had its slums, but freedom of movement within the economic structure was not inhibited by social stratification. The opportunities afforded by an expanding economy preserved the ideals of Jacksonian democracy. . . .

On the evening of April 24, 1841, a public meeting was held in the rooms of the Mercantile Library Association of Boston for the purpose of considering the plans of M. Nicholas Marie Alexandre Vattemare to encourage the international exchange of cultural materials. For almost fifteen years M. Vattemare, French actor and ventriloquist of much talent and considerable reputation, had devoted "his time, energy, and property to the introduction of his system of the international exchange of books, and, incidentally, of any products of nature or human skill which might increase knowledge in science and art." According to Josiah P. Quincy, who knew Vattemare well, the purpose of the plan was "to give the intellectual treasures of the civilized world the same dissemination and equalization which commerce [had] already given to its material ones." In Boston, as elsewhere in the United States, Vattemare found no great public libraries which might receive the books that he wished to send into the country, and the promotion of public libraries, or depositories, was a corollary of his system of international exchanges. He therefore proposed in Boston that the several local libraries, controlled by private associations, be united into one public institution. The suggestion met with an enthusiastic response, and the meeting at the Mercantile Library did not adjourn until a resolution that promised full support for "the great project" had been unanimously adopted. . . . Concerning Vattemare's ideas, Josiah Quincy, Sr., had previously written to his son: "In short I see but few obstacles, and a great advantage in the scheme proposed, and I am not for rejecting it, on the consideration that it did not originate with us. . . . We can never hope to succeed in anything, if we begin with a preconception that it is unattainable." Though one should recognize that Vattemare's enthusiasm for public library promotion was a by-product of his passion for the international exchange of books, especially government reports, the important part which his system played in public library encouragement must not be discounted. . . .

More than a decade separated the first visit to Boston of this eccentric ventriloquist and apostle of culture from the realization of his dream of a public library for the city of Boston—years during which it required the combined influence of many civic leaders to overcome the inertia of popular apathy. . . .

—From *Foundations of the Public Library,* by Jesse H. Shera (The University of Chicago Press, 1949)

Ballot Mercantile libraries were established for the use of merchants' clerks but later opened to a broader clientele. They represented one of the earliest forms of cooperation between business and libraries. This ballot for directors in the Mercantile Library of New York shows the business affiliations of the candidates. (The Smithsonian)

Taking Stock This rare share of stock in the Concord, Massachusetts, Agricultural Library is testament to the passing of the age in which libraries were stock companies. The records of this library formed early in the nineteenth century showed considerable holdings in the areas of agriculture, geology, chemistry, and botany. (The Smithsonian)

Mercantile Library

ASSOCIATION,
CLINTON HALL, ASTOR PLACE.

Regular Nominations, 1870-71.

For Directors.

M. C. D. BORDEN,
With Low, Harriman & Co.

A. B. CARPENTER,
With Leather Manufacturers' Bank.

SAMUEL PUTNAM,
With Fletcher, Harrison & Co.

EDWARD HASLER,
With the Citizens' Savings Bank.

GEORGE B. MILLS,
With Murray, Ferris & Co.

CHAS. F. ALLEN,
With the Great Western Ins. Co.

J. C. CURRIE,
With Tefft, Griswold & Kellogg.

ASHER S. MILLS,
With Hercules Mutual Life Assurance Society.

W. C. RHODES,
With Woodward, Lawrence & Co,

JOHN NICKINSON,
With A. T. Stewart & Co.

WM. A. SHERMAN,
With Bank of New York.

W. S. FLAGG,
With S. B. Chittenden & Co.

Election TUESDAY, 17th inst.
POLLS OPEN FROM 8 A. M. UNTIL 9 P. M.

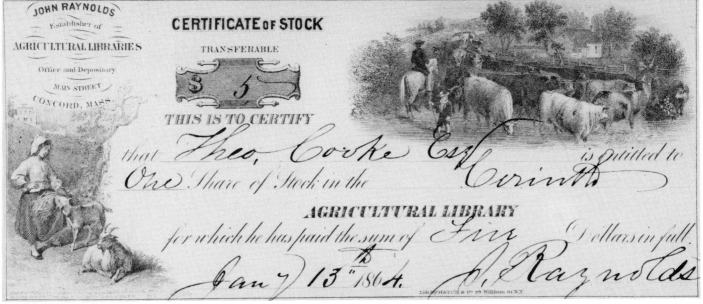

JOHN RAYNOLDS Establisher of AGRICULTURAL LIBRARIES Office and Depository MAIN STREET CONCORD, MASS.

CERTIFICATE OF STOCK

TRANSFERABLE

$5

THIS IS TO CERTIFY that *Theo. Cooke Esq* is entitled to One Share of Stock in the *Corinth* AGRICULTURAL LIBRARY for which he has paid the sum of *Five* Dollars in full.

Jany 13" 1864. *Raynolds*

Lith by HATCH & Co 29 William St N.Y.

Open Spaces If nothing else, the grand libraries of the last century featured marvelous, ornate open spaces that offered their patrons a cathedral-like atmosphere. Through prints appearing in popular magazines of the day we catch a glimpse *(right)* of the reading room of the Boston Public Library, the vestibule *(above, right)* and main hall *(over, left)* of the Cincinnati Public Library, and the Astor Library in New York *(over, right)*. The views of the Cincinnati library appeared in *Harper's Weekly* for March 21, 1874, which termed it "the largest, best-arranged and only fire-proof public library building in the country." Its ornamented glass ceiling gave the place the "proper amount of light" which even extended into the alcoves. The writer added that the alcoves at the Boston Public and Astor Libraries were "as dark as Egypt." (From *Every Saturday, Harper's Weekly,* and *Gleason's Pictorial*)

16

17

After the Fire In response to the Great Fire that swept the city of Chicago in 1871, a number of prominent people from England decided to give books to the city. Donors included Queen Victoria, Benjamin Disraeli and Robert Browning. The city put the books in an abandoned water tower that had been spared by the fire. Prior to the fire Chicago had no public library, but the British gift changed that, and the Chicago Public Library was founded in 1871. Here is a view of the temporary water tower library *(above)* and a bookplate inscribed by the Queen. The plate makes it clear that the city's English benefactors expect to see a library in the plans for the rebuilt city. (Free Library of Philadelphia and the Chicago Public Library)

PRESENTED TO

THE CITY OF CHICAGO,

TOWARDS THE FORMATION OF A FREE LIBRARY
AFTER THE GREAT FIRE OF

1871,

AS A MARK OF ENGLISH SYMPATHY,

BY *Her Majesty the Queen*
Victoria

When the United States celebrated its Centennial with a great exposition in Philadelphia, libraries had just come out of a period of great expansion. There were now 3,682 of all types, up from a mere 779 in 1850. The time was now ripe for organization, and a young dynamo named Melvil Dewey of Amherst College issued a call for a meeting of all librarians in Philadelphia in October. Among other things, the 103 delegates to the meeting took the occasion to found the American Library Association. In her *American Library Development*, Elizabeth W. Stone points out, "The formation of the Association in 1876 helped to give librarians status and *esprit de corps*, as well as practical assistance in perfecting and promoting library service."

Man of the Hour: 1876 Not only was the Centennial year witness to the birth of the American Library Association, but the beginning of *Library Journal* and the publication of the decimal classification system. All three events involved Melvil Dewey *(right)*, who had called the organizational meeting, emerged as the first editor of *Library Journal*, and created the classification system that still bears his name. He went on to found the first library school, the first state library association, and some of the first traveling libraries. He was also an advocate of the metric system and a spelling reformer—hence the variant spelling of Melville. (Library of Congress)

OCTOBER 4, 1876 PHILADELPHIA

Like . . . many other groups, the librarians decided that the Centennial year was an appropriate time to organize themselves. . . . The hundred-plus scholars found their deliberations prodded their tasks prescribed for them by a brash twenty-five-year-old, Melvil Dewey, who had just this year published his Dewey Decimal Classification. In collaboration with the aggressive editor of *Publisher's Weekly*, R. R. Bowker, Dewey also contrived to put into the hands of the librarians the first issue of the *Library Journal*, which they gratefully adopted as their official organ thereafter. As his reward for these and other labors, Dewey was able to rent an office in Boston and put a sign on the door "American Library Association, Melvil Dewey Secretary." Below that was lettered "American Metric Bureau, Melvil Dewey Secretary." And still farther down the visitor could read "Spelling Reform Association, Melvil Dewey Secretary."

"Whichever way I turn I see something that sadly needs improvement," Dewey once declared. The son of an upstate New York general storeowner, he was remembered as a youth who saved his nickels so as to buy Webster's unabridged dictionary. At Amherst College he made extra money by teaching shorthand to his fellows. During his junior year in 1873 he "devyzed the Decimal Clasification," the idea coming to him "during a long sermon by President Stearns while I lookt stedfastly at him without hearing a word." The next year, as assistant librarian at Amherst, he was in a position to test his ideas and perfect his celebrated classification. The first edition contained forty-two pages, growing to 1,647 pages a half century later.

American librarians were on the point of professionalizing themselves, Dewey or no. As of 1876 the country had 3,647 libraries with collections more than 300 books. The Library of Congress was the largest with 293,500 volumes. Harvard led the private collections with 228,000. The big problem was cataloguing. Hitherto librarians just numbered each book consecutively as it was put on the shelves, without regard to its content, and often the four conventional sizes were put in separate locations. Dewey's innovation was to assign numbers to the books, not to the shelves. By his system 0 was assigned General works, 1 Philosophy, 2 Religion, 3 Social Sciences, 4 Philology, and so forth. History, which was 9, would further be broken down into 910 Geography and Travels, 920 Biography, 930 Ancient History, and so forth. His classification, which was ahead of anything currently used in Europe and reflected an American passion for standardization and efficiency, came to be almost universally used in this country within fifty years.

Dewey had a broader view of library science than numbers on books. He put forth the slogan the Library Association later adopted: "The best reading for the largest numbers at the least cost." The idea that stirred him above all was that libraries were not for hoarding books but for getting them into the hands of readers. . . . What Dewey and other progressives had to counter this time was the attitude of such traditional custodians as the Harvard librarian who once joyfully boasted that all his books were in place except two in the possession of Professor Agassiz, which he was just then on his way to fetch. The newer library philosophy would be propagated systematically a decade later when Dewey established the first school of library science at Columbia University.

—From *The Hundredth Year: The United States in 1876,* by John D. Bergamini (G. P. Putnam's Sons, New York, 1976)

Pyramid Members of the library staff at the Minneapolis Public Library in 1892. The woman at the top is Gratia Countryman, who would become head librarian twelve years later. (Minneapolis Public Library)

Dewey with Students Although a few have recently criticized Dewey for a degree of condescension toward women, he was a crusader for the admission of women to library training courses and for their equality in the profession. An oft-repeated quote from Dewey: "To my thinking, a great librarian must have a clear head, a strong hand, and above all, a great heart. Such shall be greatest among librarians; and when I look into the future, I am inclined to think that most of the men who will achieve this greatness will be women." Here he is shown with the library science class of 1888 at Columbia University. (ALA Archives)

LIBRARY ST. MARY'S COLLEGE

Ladies and Linoleum These two views of the new Minneapolis Public Library, which opened in 1889, typify the latest in amenities of the time. The drawing is of the ladies' reading room, and the photograph shows the main reading room, whose appointments were described at the time of the opening: "There are tables and chairs of such designs as secure the largest amount of comfort to all who have occasion to use them. These are conveniently disposed and, as the floor is laid in linoleum, they can be moved easily and noiselessly." (Minneapolis Public Library)

THE PROFESSION IN 1876

The time has at last come when a librarian may, without assumption, speak of his occupation as a profession. And, more, a better time has come—perhaps we should say is coming, for it still has many fields to conquer. The best librarians are no longer men of merely negative virtues. They are positive, aggressive characters, standing in the front rank of the educators of their communities, side by side with the preachers and the teachers. The people are more and more getting their incentives and ideas from the printed page. There are more readers and fewer listeners, and men who move and lead the world are using the press more and the platform less. It needs no argument to prove that reading matter can be distributed better and more cheaply through lending libraries than in any other way, and we shall assume, what few will presume to dispute, that the largest influence over the people is the printed page and that this influence may be wielded most surely and strongly through our libraries.

From the first, libraries have commanded great respect, and much has been written of their priceless worth; but the opinion has been largely prevalent that a librarian was a keeper only, and had done his full duty if he preserved the books from loss, and to a reasonable extent from the worms. There have been noble exceptions to this rule, but still it is a modern idea that librarians should be more than this. It is not now enough that the books are cared for properly, are well arranged, are never lost. It is not enough that he can, when asked, give advice as to the best books in his collection on any given subject. All these things are indispensable, but all these are not enough for our ideal. He must see that his library contains, as far as possible, the best books on the best subjects, regarding carefully the wants of his special community. Then, having the best books, he must create among his people, his pupils, a desire to read these books. He must put every facility in the way of readers, so that they shall be led on from good to better. He must teach them how, after studying their own wants, they may themselves select their reading wisely. Such a librarian will find enough who are ready to put themselves under his influence and direction, and, if competent and enthusiastic, he may soon largely shape the reading, and through it the thought, of his whole community.

The time is come when we are not astonished to find the ablest business talents engaged in the management of a public library. Not that we have less scholarship, but that we have more life. The passive has become active, and we look for a throng of people going in and out of library doors as in the markets and the stores. There was a time when libraries were opened only at intervals, and visitors came occasionally, as they come sometimes to a deserted castle or to a haunted house. Now many of our libraries are as accessible as our post-offices, and the number of new libraries founded has been so great that in an ordinary town we no longer ask, "Have you a library?" but "Where is your library?" as we might ask where is your school-house, or your post-office, or your church?

—From an article by Melvil Dewey in the first issue of *Library Journal*, September 30, 1876

Incombustible Ideal When the Central Library Building for Chicago opened its doors on October 11, 1897, it fulfilled the ideal that obtained during the period, which was to create a palace for the masses. With the Great Fire still in mind, it was intended to be fireproof. Besides the exterior *(right)*, we see newspaper reading stands *(below)* on the Randolph Street entrance to the building. (Chicago Public Library)

New Realms Chicago, like other big-city libraries, was finding new areas in which to serve readers. Deposit stations were set up around the city, and books were taken to drugstores, churches, factories, and other locations in the neighborhoods. Shown here are the wagons used to carry books to the stations *(top)*, a letter *(above)* concerning books provided to the Cook County House of Corrections, and the next step *(right)*, a Branch Reading Room. The reading room shown is at Jane Addams' Hull House. (Chicago Public Library and Jane Addams Memorial Collection, University Library, University of Illinois at Chicago)

WHAT IT WAS LIKE IN 1885

Picture to yourselves, if you will, a typical city library in, say, the year 1885. The building is dingy, if dignified, dimly lighted, its walls painted the ubiquitous muddy buff considered suitable for a public institution. Within is a desk shutting off the sacred book collection, which extends back into a dark crypt called the "stacks." Behind the desk sits a self-contained librarian, perhaps a bespectacled little gentleman, perhaps one of the old maids of popular fancy, perhaps a scared youngster with her hair in pigtails, pinchhitting for one of the former; and in the outskirts a boy or girl "runner," whose duty it is to procure the wanted book from the stacks for the would-be reader, who fills out the necessary information from the card catalogue, and hands his slip to the librarian, but never penetrates the closed gates to the books beyond. Perhaps at one side there is a reading and reference room with—yes—a "Silence" sign prominently displayed.

One of the most forward-looking steps taken by the public library was to remove the gate, push back the desk, and open the book section to the public. Today every small library and many moderately large ones display the majority of their books on open shelves. Even the largest libraries have open-shelf rooms where their collections of current literature are available to all readers. Yet this obviously democratic move was made tentatively, against the severest opposition by many conservative librarians and library boards. Some of the reasons for this opposition were logical and remain today serious factors in the care and protection of books. The loss and mutilation of expensive books and the wear and tear on rare books due to over-handling are important considerations which account for much of the present-day protection of these two classes behind closed book shelves. Other reasons for the reluctance to place books on open shelves, such as noise and disorder, or the likelihood of misplacement in returning books to shelves, even the danger of infection, which was a cause of serious dispute, seem to us today trivial and a bit old-fashioned.

Two pioneers in this movement were William F. Brett, of the Cleveland Public Library, and John Cotton Dana, then of the Denver, Colorado, Public Library. When the fine new building of the Boston Public Library opened in 1890 with a large room displaying books on open shelves the tide turned against the conservatives. Opposition waned and the early twentieth century saw the open-shelf policy in public libraries firmly established.

Developments which indicated a trend of thought startlingly new at that time were those which occurred in the library's attitude to children and the increasing attention given to their needs. An important phase of this development was the specialized book service offered by a number of librarians to their city schools, a policy which met with hearty favor, and which spread quite widely from about 1885 to 1914. That this service was appreciated as a valuable adjunct to teaching is evidenced by its influence in promoting the establishment of libraries within the schools. Today school libraries constitute one of the most important library groups. Moreover, coordinated reading and reference service by public libraries and schools working together toward the enrichment of class room programs offers a promising new avenue of library progress.

—From *The Public Library in American Life,* by Ernestine Rose (Columbia University Press, 1954)

If there was a moment that symbolized the great strides that had been made in the progress of the library in the nineteenth century, it was the opening of the new Library of Congress in 1897.

First Floor When this picture was taken in 1891, the building was still six years from opening. Thousands of photographs were taken during its construction. By the time it was completed, it was considered the most lavish display of stone, metal, and glass ever seen in America. (Library of Congress)

Crowd Scene A few months before the new building opened, this drawing appeared in *Harper's Weekly.* It was used to emphasize the congestion of the old library. The bearded gentleman at the right is Ainsworth Rand Spofford, the sixth Librarian. One of Spofford's many accomplishments was to make the national copyright office part of the Library. (L.C.)

Stacks The degree to which ornamentation was part of the new library is seen in this drawing—one of 1,600 plans and drawings used—of an area that is off limits to the public. It is odd to see the shelves bare because they have been filling ever since. Currently the Library uses 535 miles of shelves to hold over 80 million books and other items. (L.C.)

Cards This photograph of the old card division suggests the enormity of the task involved in the Library's cataloging work. The main catalog became the world's largest with some 60 million individual cards but is now being phased out in favor of its electronic counterpart. (L.C.)

Service to the Blind One special feature of the new building was a special reading room for the blind. This effort has grown to the point where upwards of 600,000 blind people take advantage of the Library's services. (L.C.)

Students Although the primary mission of the Library was to serve Congress, it has always functioned as if it were a public library. This became even more evident after the opening of the new building. Less than a year after it opened, the hours were expanded to allow the public to use it on weekends and in the evening, and the Librarian of Congress could report that it was on its way to becoming "a bureau of information consulted by people from all sections." These extended hours remained intact until 1986, when they were curtailed by the force of the Gramm–Rudman–Hollings budget-reduction act. In this picture of the new reading room, students are shown using the library. The man standing is Herbert Putnam, who became Librarian of Congress in 1899. (L.C.)

In Its Glory All 800 tons of books were transferred from the Capitol to the new building in wheelbarrows and wagons for the opening. The final cost was $6,032,124.54—some $200,000 less than had been appropriated for the building by Congress. When it was completed, the point was made that it had been built to hold all earthly knowledge under one roof. By 1938 a large Annex was added; in 1960 still another new building was dedicated. (L.C.)

(E-24.)

Rare Book Room This reading room is modeled after Independence Hall in Philadelphia. Today the collection of the Rare Book Division contains more than 500,000 items, including books, manuscripts, broadsides, and pamphlets. (L.C.)

Main Reading Room *(Opposite)* This famous room vaults 125 feet from floor to dome. At the center is the central desk, which serves an endless parade of patrons. (L.C.)

Great Hall This drawing by an employee of the Library shows the point where tours of the building have traditionally started. Years later a newspaperman was to write of its splendor, "Entering its main floor the visitor is presented with such a vision of richly hued marble, bright mosaics, classic carving, and heroic sculpture that the Capitol across the street seems like a spartan cave." (L.C.)

Hallowed Chamber When the Supreme Court vacated its old chamber in the Capitol in 1860, it became the Law Library of the Library of Congress and continued as such for the next ninety years. This photograph shows the Law Library as it appeared in 1895. (L.C.)

In Reserve Coming up on the turn of the century, New York City decided that it would remove the Croton Reservoir to make room for its grand new library at the corner of Fifth Avenue and 42nd Street. In 1895 the Astor and Lenox Libraries and the Tilden Trust merged to form what thereafter would be formally called the New York Public Library, Astor, Lenox and Tilden Foundations. (New York Public Library)

Books Behind Cages These two views of the Denver Public Library at LaVeta Place show the Children's Department *(right)* and the main loan desk *(opposite)*. They show the customary cage from which books were dispensed before advocates of open shelves made and won their case. Ironically, these images showing closed stacks are at one of the first systems to do away with them. Cleveland and Boston were other open-stack pioneers. Denver was the second place in America to open a children's reading room, which it created from its former ''ladies' reading room.'' (Denver Public Library)

LITTLE ROOM
FOR CHILDREN
1803 TO
THE END OF
THE CENTURY

. . . In the early part of the nineteenth century there were a number of individuals who donated either books or tiny endowments, presumably in the hope that a municipality might pick up the rest of the "tab." In 1803 Caleb Bingham . . . contributed 150 titles to his home town (Salisbury, Connecticut), to be made freely available to children between the ages of nine and sixteen. He left to others the obligation to care for and distribute these books; in 1810 the citizens in town meeting did vote financial aid to the Bingham Library for Youth—perhaps the first such library in the United States to receive support from a municipality. . . . in 1835, there was the bequest of a physician in West Cambridge (now Arlington), Massachusetts. He left one hundred dollars for a library that would diffuse "useful knowledge and the Christian virtues" to children. After a year the town voted to appropriate forty dollars to make books free to adults as well, and this generosity marked the beginning of what is now the Arlington Public Library! In the 1850s a Colonel James Anderson of Allegheny, Pennsylvania, made his library of 400 volumes accessible to working boys. One of the urchins was Andrew Carnegie who would later erect a monument to Anderson and would contribute much of his own wealth to the building of public libraries.

In spite of these estimable individual efforts, in the waning years of the nineteenth century there had been little progress toward the goal of providing books for the children of the land. In 1876, the Centennial Year, the United States Government published a voluminous report on public libraries. The volume had an index of thirteen closely printed, double-column pages—with not a single entry under "child" or "children." Service to youth, in alcoves or rooms or other facilities of public institutions, first appeared in 1885. The initial one seems to have been a children's library established in that year by Emily Hanaway, the principal of the primary department of Grammar School No. 28 in New York City. The first public librarian to do something for children who were roaming the streets was Mrs. Minerva Sanders of Pawtucket, Rhode Island. She was something of a "radical" who believed in a people's library; she had introduced open shelves, had encouraged workingmen to come to her institution, and was most interested in children at a time when they were considered noisy nuisances. In 1887 Sanders welcomed youngsters to a corner of the reading room where she had provided four tables and chairs, lowered because she had ordered a large segment of the legs cut off; the facility seated seventy children, and there were shelves nearby stocked with books of interest to the young. The boys and girls responded by dubbing her with the affectionate sobriquet of "Auntie Sanders." In 1890 the Public Library in Brookline, Massachusetts, opened in its basement the first reading room especially for children; three years later the Minneapolis Public Library found space in a corridor for children; the next year the Denver Public Library appropriated a "ladies' reading room" and changed it into a children's library with books within easy reach on low shelves. Shortly thereafter a separate children's reading room became a part of every well-constructed and properly operated public library. No longer would children be served solely by sending collections of books to the schools. They were now being recognized as part of the public—needing their own quarters, their own book collections, and a specially trained staff to serve them.

—From *Open Shelves and Open Minds*, by C. H. Cramer, (Case Western Reserve University Press, 1972)

I THIS WAY IN.

Work with Children The Aguilar Free
Library was created in 1886 by a group of
philanthropic Jews who wanted to create
a public library system for the teeming
lower East Side. When it merged with
the New York Public Library in 1903, it
had four branches of its own. In the later
years of the nineteenth century, libraries
began to actively serve the masses of
immigrants coming into the country.
(NYPL)

Service to Children It was common in the nineteenth century to prohibit children under the age of twelve or fourteen from public libraries and children's reading rooms were unheard of until the first one opened in Brookline, Massachusetts, in 1890. The Cleveland Public Library was one that moved quickly into this new area. Dramatic visual evidence of this concern remains in these photographs, which show the story hour at the Perkins Branch (1898, *opposite, top*) the Juvenile alcove at the Main Branch (1898, *right*), another story hour (1900, *below, right*) and a home-deposit library on Hill Street (ca. 1900, *opposite, bottom*). (Cleveland Public Library)

1900–1920
BUILDING
BLOCKS

At the turn of the century the library movement first began to experience trends and developments that continue to be important to this day. New freedoms—open shelves, the right to take home more than one book, and falling age barriers—spread beyond pioneering libraries. Growth was the order of the day. Beginning in 1898, there was an active movement to set up county library systems. Branch libraries, which had started to appear in a few of the larger cities in the 1890s, were taking hold elsewhere, and small deposit-station libraries could be found everywhere. Increasingly, libraries were working to serve special groups, ranging from immigrants to the handicapped, while smaller and smaller towns were declaring their need for a free, public library. In short, the public library was beginning to move out into the community. As the editors of *Public Libraries* observed in 1901: "Nothing seems more certain . . . than that the future will see, in every city of any considerable size, a system of public libraries installed in numerous buildings in various parts of the town, in much the same manner as the public school system is managed today. The day of one colossal building, serving the people inadequately, and standing more for a place of exhibition and the resort of scholars of leisure than a people's university is certainly passing." All of this progress was to be helped to no small degree by Andrew Carnegie.

Harbinger Andrew Carnegie once said that his gifts to libraries fell into two periods: the "retail" period, which ran from 1886 to 1898, and the "wholesale" period that followed. He began all of this with a gift of a million dollars to Pittsburgh to pay for a main library and seven branches. This picture was taken in 1900 in the new Carnegie Library of Pittsburgh, as the "wholesale" period was getting started. (Carnegie Library of Pittsburgh)

Before the Lions A significant development of the early years of the new century was the building of the New York Public Library at Fifth Avenue and 42nd Street. Now it is known as the Central Research Library of the New York Public Library, but by whatever name, it stands as one of the great libraries of the world. This photograph shows the extent of work that had been completed in 1904. The cornerstone had been laid in 1902, and work continued until it opened in 1911, at which time it was the largest marble structure in the country. (NYPL)

Checking In More and more the large libraries were finding that they had to develop increasingly complex and labor-intensive systems for handling books. At the Carnegie Library of Pittsburgh books are being checked in at a station at the fourth stack. (CLP)

DEWEY ON THE FUTURE OF THE PUBLIC LIBRARIAN 1903

The future of the public librarian is largely dependent on the future of the book, the library, the reader, and the trustees—the factors with which he has largely to deal. Recent investigations on large numbers of children have shown that the chief influence on the life of the child, and through him on the citizen of the future came not from father, mother, teacher, or school, but from the reading of childhood. The librarian of the future, who guides more than any other force the reading of the community, therefore, holds in his hands the longest lever with which man has ever pried.

The old librarian stayed at home, usually both from preference and necessity. Now, and still more in the future, he travels, broadens his horizon, utilizes the experiments of others, and accomplishes more for his constituency with the time and money at his disposal by keeping in touch with what others are doing.

The librarian of the future in all the larger institutions will become a faculty just as the single teacher has developed into the college faculty, and he will use labor-saving devices and appliances wherever they are found practicable in saving time or money, so that we may fairly say that he will do his work, not by hand, but by machinery. Telephones, typewriters, card systems, fountain pens, and every practical aid will be brought into play as freely as they would in a manufactory or commercial office, for the librarian of the future will break loose entirely from the mediaeval traditions that seem to make it unprofessional for him to study minute economies. In the library, the reference librarian, himself a very recent and very valuable invention for helping the public, must be differentiated by subjects, for the demands of the public are so exacting that no human being could even pretend to be thoroughly familiar with the whole range of literature on a great variety of topics. The great libraries are assigning specialists to one department after another, as public demands warrant and we are developing in the national and in the leading states, and great central libraries, a system of library faculties destined to revolutionize some of our professional work.

Librarians are rapidly taking on their proper functions as book experts for their various constituencies. But the librarian is rapidly outgrowing the idea that he is concerned with books alone. The public pays its money, not to dignify books as such, but because it wishes information, or, still better, inspiration or innocent recreation, afforded in the best and cheapest way. This is oftenest through books, but pictures, specimens, classes, and lectures, and other means are found sometimes to be more effective or desirable. The library of the future is the recognized head of all these agencies, designed for old and young alike, to be had at home while engaged in other duties, as contrasted with the school education, designed only for the young for a limited course, and for those whose main business is to go to school.

—Melvil Dewey, from Volume 8 of the periodical *Public Libraries*

Great Hall Besides displaying one of the nation's more spectacular reading rooms, this turn-of-the-century stereoview of the Boston Public Library features a black patron. Elsewhere in America it would be sixty years before a picture like this could be taken. (Library of Congress)

Fire Stations Deposit stations were becoming such an important element of urban library systems that by 1909 the Chicago Public Library could report that small satellite stations accounted for two-thirds of the system's entire circulation. There seemed to be no limit to the variety of places that a deposit station could be located. These turn-of-the-century photographs from Cleveland show stations on the fireboat *Clevelander (opposite top)* and at Engine House Number 2 *(opposite bottom)*. (Cleveland Public Library)

The impact of Andrew Carnegie on the American library was profound. He granted money for the construction of 1,679 public library buildings in 1,412 communities across the nation and also built another 830 overseas. Ranging from those for the 52 branch libraries he gave the city of New York to those for libraries in the small towns of the South and Midwest, his grants were felt in all parts of the nation. Rhode Island was the only state not to get a Carnegie building. The bequests came at the right time—library expansion was the order of the day, and it was fortunate that one man possessed the wealth to make sure it could occur.

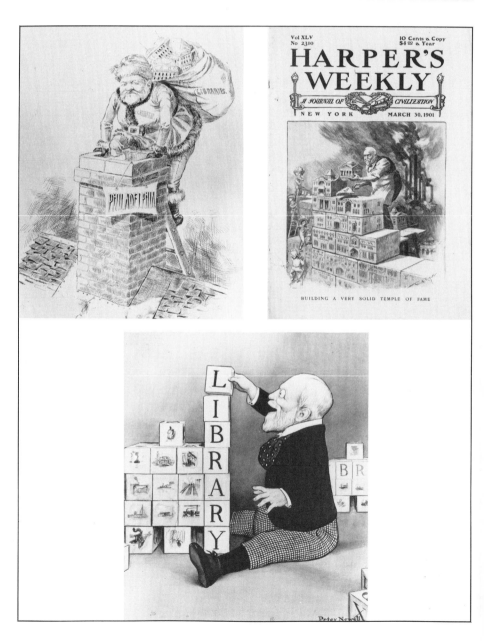

Library Santa Cartoonists seemed unable to resist trying to capture Andrew Carnegie in his role as the great builder of libraries. Shown are three examples: a cartoon *(top left)* from the *Philadelphia Inquirer* of January 8, 1903, rendered shortly after his gift of $1.5 million to the city of Philadelphia (Free Library of Philadelphia), the cover of *Harper's Weekly* of March 30, 1901 *(top right)*, and a cartoon of Carnegie *(bottom)* by Peter Newell from 1903 (Houghton Library, Harvard). The Newell cartoon was drawn for *Harper's Weekly*, where it appeared in April of 1903 with the following caption:
Andrew Carnegie
We men are only lusty boys
Though snowy be our locks;
To Skobo's master still enjoys
To sit and play with blocks.
(Cooper-Hewitt Museum)

Prime Examples If nothing else, the Carnegie gifts allowed the architects of the time to express themselves in a variety of styles. Despite the common perception, the libraries did not all look alike. When the Cooper-Hewitt Museum in New York mounted a major exhibition in 1985 on the architecture of the Carnegie libraries, a statement at the beginning of the show said in part, "it is difficult to characterize the Carnegie libraries as a group. The program was so vast and the circumstances for which these buildings were designed were so varied that perhaps it can only be said that in the aggregate they reflect the extraordinary richness of American architecture at the turn of the century. . . ." The St. Louis Public Library *(right),* built between 1908 and 1909 at a cost of $81,365, and the Savannah Public Library *(below),* built between 1915 and 1916 for $87,000, were two of many handsome city libraries paid for by Carnegie. (Smithsonian Institution Traveling Exhibition Service)

FATHER ANDY'S SOCIAL IDEAS EARLY TWENTIETH CENTURY

"Father Andy," as a grateful nation nicknamed Andrew Carnegie, arranged his library philanthropies so as not to encourage the charity psychology which hampered free library progress in New York City. His system gave little comfort to local politicians who were shirking community responsibility while waiting for some wealthy patron to appear with funds sufficient to create and support a library. Believing the educational function in a democracy to be the peculiar province of the state, he limited his own activities to the donation of buildings, and required a guarantee from each municipality that a library would be established and adequately financed by annual appropriations. Carnegie's role in the library movement was not that of an initiator; it was rather that of a stimulant to an organism which might have rested long on a plateau had it not been spurred on to greater heights. The free library had started on a firm foundation in New England and doubtless would in time have embedded itself in the public consciousness of the entire nation. However, at the time Carnegie appeared on the scene with his novel scheme of helping him who first helps himself, the retarding influence of "waiting for a Lenox" was making itself felt in many frustrated local library movements. His philanthropy was designed in such a way that the officers of municipalities would have to justify themselves annually to their citizens for not accepting the well-publicized standing offer of a public library building. . . .

The great ironmaster consistently eschewed any form of giving which might encourage a relaxation of effort on the part of recipients of his gifts. Gifts which had the taint of pauperism, thought he, would stifle that initiative which lay at the foundation of our glorious republic. A library of the people had to be supported by the people. The independent masses must remain independent in their upward movement of social betterment. This state of things could be maintained in the instance of public libraries by a wholesale system of bribery. The building which a community got for nothing—and, said Carnegie, people will take anything for nothing—was actually bait to ensnare holders of the public purse.

Popular initiative, participation and control were the desired aims; for they were basic to America's fluid, evolutionary social organization. . . . Parts of his speech before a group of Brooklyn citizens are in point:

> Surely there should be little trouble in bringing this matter before the voters, the masses of the people, and obtaining their strong support to a movement to press authorities to act according to the authority given, because no class in the community is to be benefited so clearly and so fully as the great mass of the people, the wage-earners, the laborers, the manual toilers.

> The free library is the library of the working classes, and I am persuaded that all that is necessary for you, who testify by your presence tonight your interest in the question, for the good of others rather than your own, to do is, to appoint a body of those most zealous among you to visit the various workshops, to obtain the signature of every industrious toiler you approach to a petition. . . .

—From *Arsenals of a Democratic Culture,* by Sidney Ditzion (American Library Association, 1947)

Oases If the large, urban Carnegie libraries were imposing, it was in the smaller cities and towns where the Carnegie gifts seemed to underscore the enormity of the bequests and their influence. For one thing, there were so many of them and they sometimes appeared in small, isolated places where no other building in town held a candle to the new library. These eight smaller libraries, shown on postcards, were located in eight different states and are but a modest attempt to do justice to the variety of sites and styles. Shown are libraries in Rockwell City, Iowa *(top)*; Selma, Alabama *(center)*; Winston-Salem, North Carolina *(bottom)*; Dover, New Hampshire *(overleaf, top)*; Riverside, California *(overleaf, center)*; Danville, Illinois *(overleaf, bottom)*; Douglas, Wyoming *(overleaf, opposite top)*; and Coshocton, Ohio *(overleaf, opposite center)*. A picture of the Riverside Library appeared in an exhibit at the Cooper-Hewitt Museum with the following notation: "One of the loveliest of the many Carnegie libraries in California designed in the Mission Revival style, this building was demolished in the early 1960s." (Author's collection)

49

CARNEGIE PUBLIC LIBRARY. DOVER. N.H.

CARNEGIE LIBRARY, RIVERSIDE, CAL.
VISITED BY PRESIDENT ROOSEVELT

Carnegie
Public
Library,
Danville, Ill.

Carnegie Library, Coshocton, Ohio

Boasting Possession of a Carnegie library became a point of considerable local pride. One manifestation of this was that almost all of them ended up as the subjects of postcards, which were used in great numbers by local residents to brag about the new library. These four *(bottom right and overleaf)* were typical.

PUBLIC LIBRARY, PORTLAND, ORE.

Carnegie Library, Connellsville, Pa.

Carnegie Library, Homestead, Pa.

THE BIRTH OF THE BOOK WAGON 1905

At the close of the year 1904 as has been seen before there were 66 stations in the country and 30 of these were off the line of either railroad, trolley or stage. (This was before the days of buses and automobiles for all.) And consequently the janitor with a hired horse and concord wagon was pressed into the service to carry the cases back and forth. On an average he made three trips a week. It was then that the idea of a wagon designed especially for this purpose began to ferment in the mind of the Librarian. The visits of the janitor had already done much to establish cordial relations between the Library and its patrons.

Would not a "Library Wagon," the outward and visible sign of the service for which the Library stood, do much more in cementing friendship? Would the upkeep of the wagon after the first cost be much more than the present method? Is not Washington County with its good roads especially well adapted for testing an experiment of this kind, for the geography of the County is such that it could be comfortably covered by well planned routes. These and other aspects of the plan were laid before the Board of Trustees—who approved of the idea, and forthwith the librarian began interviewing wagon makers and trying to elucidate her ideas with pen and pencil. The first wagon, when finished with shelves on the outside and a place for storage of cases in the center resembled somewhat a cross between a grocer's delivery wagon and the tin peddlers cart of bygone New England days.

Filled with an attractive collection of books and drawn by two horses, with Mr. Joshua Thomas the janitor both holding the reins and dispensing the books, it started on its travels in April 1905. No mention of the early book wagon is complete without the introduction of Mr. Thomas—a native of Washington County—a veteran of the War between the States. After the war he drove through the county regularly buying up butter, eggs and country produce for the Hagerstown market. In this way he learned every road and byway in the County and was known by all the residents, unconsciously being prepared for this later undertaking. Absolutely loyal to the institution he served, a man of much native intelligence and a good fighter, he found a use for all these qualities, for the conservative element in the country was inclined to look askance at this radical departure in library service. The Library owes much to the good work done by him in those early years. But in August 1910 the original Book Wagon was destroyed. While crossing the Norfolk and Western Railroad track at St. James a freight train ran into it leaving literally nothing but fragments. For the remainder of the year and for the year 1911 work through the wagon was perforce suspended.

—From *The Story of the Washington County Free Library*, by Mary Lemist Titcomb (Hagerstown, Maryland, Chamber of Commerce, 1951)

First A potent new idea emerged in 1905 at the Washington County Free Library in Hagerstown, Maryland. The library had been doing its best to serve a number of outlying deposit stations by train and trolley, which ran throughout the largely rural county. In 1904 the library bought a horse and wagon to reach other stations, but in 1905 it occurred to Mary Lemist Titcomb, Librarian of the Washington County Library from 1901 to 1931, that the wagon, rather than a mere delivery vehicle, could actually be a library unit itself, with books circulating from shelves mounted in cabinets on the sides of the wagon. The bookmobile was born. It is shown here before it was demolished by a Norfolk & Western locomotive in a 1910 mishap (the driver and both horses survived). (Washington County Free Library)

Second First As if it were not enough to have put the nation's first horse-drawn book wagon on the road, Washington County moved ahead and created the first automotive bookmobile in America. This took place in 1912. This picture shows the handsome new vehicle, an International Harvester Autowagon with a specially built body for carrying books. (Washington County Free Library)

THE WOMAN LIBRARY WORKER 1900–1920

By 1900 Employment Opportunities for middle-class women had greatly expanded. The college-educated or intellectually inclined women who had once chosen a career in library service became increasingly reluctant to accept the low wages and prestige accorded to librarians. Librarians, by 1912, were commonly recognized to receive less pay than teachers and to have longer working hours. Meanwhile, social work in the cities had become an idealized mission for ambitious spinsters; women welfare workers trebled in number between 1910 and 1920. A Minneapolis survey in 1918 revealed that 42.6 per cent of librarians received less than $900 annually, whereas only 29.3 per cent of social workers and 17.2 per cent of teacher did so. Almost 10 per cent of social workers earned over $2,100 per year, in contrast to one per cent of librarians. In the 1870s and 1880s, societal prejudices had led many women to shrink from work in the competitive business world. By 1920 the expanding fields of journalism, clerical work, and sales work offered new and relatively well paid jobs to middle-class women. In 1917 the graduates of Pratt Institute Library School who entered library employment received an annual wage of $845. Those graduates who began business or government careers could expect to earn an average yearly salary of $1,177. A vicious cycle was thus established by the 1920s. The nature of library work did not attract men, and salaries remained low because they were paid to women.

In the first decades of the new century the majority of women library workers were employed as assistants. In library literature between 1900 and 1920 there is abundant evidence of the dissatisfaction of head librarians with their staffs. References to assistants are singularly carping in nature. There is frequent mention of the staff's distressing lack of intelligence, accuracy, education, efficiency, motivation, and amiability. Assistants in turn, in their rare appearances in print, seem to be equally resentful of their low prestige, inadequate salary, and monotonous work.

This growing tension in the library field is an important indication of the changing nature of women's opportunities in the working world. As a living wage became available to middle-class women in other fields, the quality of library workers slowly declined. The head librarian was increasingly forced to recruit women assistants with inadequate preliminary education, many of whom were very young or intellectually unsuited to the work. Library employment across the nation became, for most women, temporary work between graduation from the public school and marriage. The *Library Journal* held the dubious distinction of being probably the only professional journal in the country that ran a regular "marriage column."

Because so much of the assistant's work was strictly routine monotony, a constant effort was necessary to incite enthusiasm for the job. Arthur Bostwick claimed that catalogue filing, pasting labels, and addressing postcards had high professional implications. "A label pasted awry may ruin the library's reputation . . . ; a mis-sent card may cause trouble to dozens of one's fellow assistants. Routine work is dull only when one does not understand it[s] purport."

—From *Apostles of Culture: The Public Librarian and American Society, 1876–1920,* by Dee Garrison (The Free Press, 1979)

Library Life The Carnegie bequest to Washington, D.C., provided for a fine new central library that was finished in 1903. Like other new central facilities, it was not long before it had turned into a beehive of activity. While many photographs of this period survive, not many express the level of activity that these three from Washington, D.C., do, taken between 1905 and 1908. We see the children's room *(right)*, a line at the return desk *(below)*, and the cataloging area *(opposite, top;* Washingtoniana Room, Martin Luther King Memorial Library)

Community Centers Increasingly
libraries were being used for more than
the circulation of books. In becoming
administrators of "the people's
university," librarians encouraged or
sponsored lectures, classes, meetings,
clubs, and concerts. Recreation was
joining education as a proper function of
the library. This picture shows an
outdoor story hour sponsored by the
Cleveland Public Library. (Cleveland
Public Library)

In the South Two undated photographs from the American Library Association Archives show aspects of library life below the Mason–Dixon line in the early part of the century. One shows the Children's Room *(right)* at the Atlanta Public Library, while the second *(below)* shows the Tuskegee Institute Library. Both, incidentally, were Carnegie beneficiaries: Tuskegee received a $25,000 grant for library construction in 1900 and Atlanta got $202,000 in 1898. (ALA Archives, University of Illinois)

Into the Factories This rolling library was placed in the National Cash Register Company in Dayton, Ohio. The factory floor was a common location for deposit libraries. (ALA Archives, University of Illinois)

"Door of Opportunity" Gratia Countryman of the Minneapolis Public Library looked at the condition of the unemployed in her city, many of them immigrants, and decided that they should have a reading room where they could congregate to read and relax. This special room opened in 1910 in the area of the city where these unfortunate men lived in cheap hotels and flophouses. She declared it a "door of opportunity for all such as these" and noted that many of the men lived in places which were so mean that they were denied "the privilege of a chair." (Minneapolis Public Library)

Services to Children In the early days of the twentieth century one of the leading forces in the field of children's librarianship was The New York Public Library. Much of this reputation could be attributed directly to Annie Carroll Moore, who took charge of children's services in 1906 and immediately removed *all* age restrictions for children using the library—a radical departure for the time. She improved the collections and turned the children's rooms in the branches into a setting for storytelling, festivals, exhibits, and clubs. She used the branch children's rooms to celebrate the ethnic background of the neighborhood rather than "Americanize" the neighborhood children. Although lacking specific information to identify the branch at which they were taken, these photographs from the New York Public Library vividly reflect of era. (NYPL)

Storytelling In this picture taken by the great photographer Lewis Hine, the New York Public Library's Supervisor of Storytelling, Anne Cogswell Tyler, is shown with a reading club for older girls at one of the branches. (Art, Prints and Photographs Division, New York Public Library, Astor, Lenox, and Tilden Foundation)

On Top of the World Children on the roof garden of the Hamilton Fish Park branch of the New York Public Library in 1911. (NYPL)

New York Landmark When it opened on May 23, 1911, the *New York Times* called the New York Public Library "one of the few beautiful buildings in a city of ugly architecture." This is how it looked 75 years later, which is very much the way it looked when it opened save for the skyscrapers that have grown up around it. In 1971 Ada Louise Huxtable wrote that "in spite of its formal grandeur, the experience of the building is intimate and emotional. In spite of its scale, it is never cold or tiring." (NYPL)

Icon Patience is one of the two guardian lions in front of the New York Public Library. Patience sits on the south, or downtown, side of the building and Fortitude sits on the north. Their original nicknames were "Leo Lenox" and "Leo Astor," after two of the library's founders—James Lenox and John Jacob Astor—but were given their present names by Fiorello LaGuardia in the 1930s because patience and fortitude were the qualities "New Yorkers most needed to survive the Depression." Each December they are adorned with huge wreaths. The appearance of the wreaths are said to signify the beginning of the Christmas shopping season on Fifth Avenue. The lions have appeared in countless cartoons, drawings, poems, and in at least one play, a work by John Guare in which they eat a librarian. (NYPL)

Stacks This cross-section (*overleaf far right*) of the new library appeared in *Scientific American* on the occasion of its opening. It shows the seven layers of bookstacks that lay below the main reading room. With only minor modifications this system of book handling remains in operation today. (NYPL)

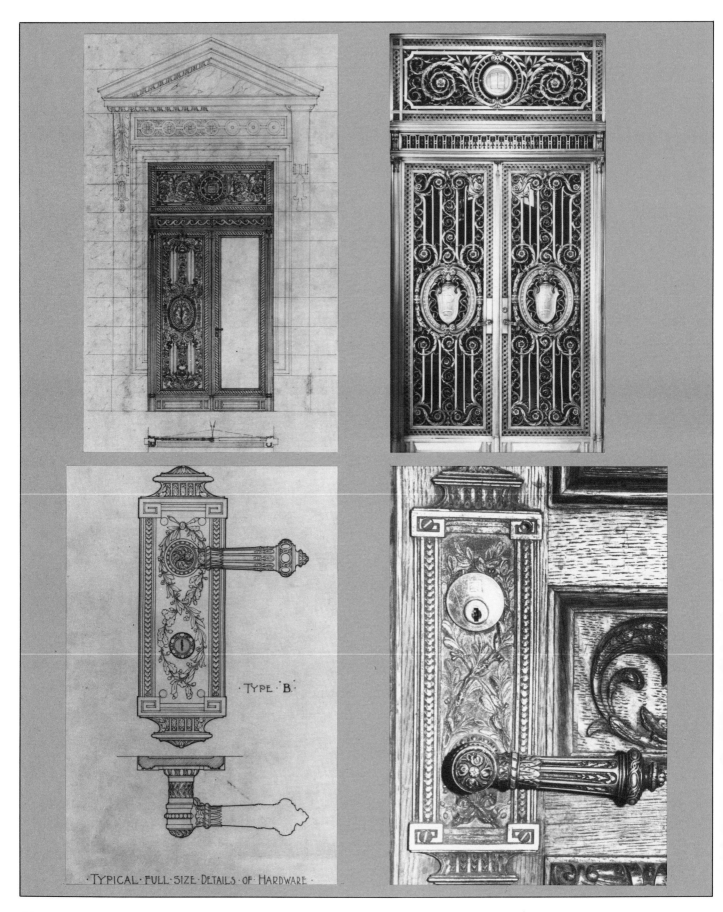

·TYPE·B·

·TYPICAL·FULL·SIZE·DETAILS·OF·HARDWARE·

Details If there was one thing about which the critics of the new building were in almost complete agreement, it was that its marble interior was superb and the detailing beyond reproach. These architectural drawings from the original 6,000 used for the project show a few of these details. Shown *(opposite, top)* are doors for the library's exhibition hall, a figure from the third-floor ceiling *(right)*, and *(opposite bottom)* two views of the doorknobs designed for the library. (NYPL © 1986 by Anne Day)

Catalog Shown here just after it had opened in 1911, the public catalog room of the New York Public Library *(below)*. It and the adjoining main reading room were heralded as two of the most impressive spaces of their kind in the world. This room closed in 1985 for restoration and reopened at the beginning of 1986. Computer terminals had been installed and the 9,000 card drawers were gone. One interesting aspect of the restoration was that considerable space was found behind the wall paneling for air conditioning, heating, and the cables required for the new electronics. It was as if the original architects had allowed room for innovations unknown to them. (NYPL)

LENIN ON THE "PROFANE USE OF LIBRARIANSHIP" 1913

What can be done for public education:

In western countries a number of unhealthy prejudices are widespread from which Holy Mother Russia is free. There, for example, they hold that great public libraries, with hundreds of thousands and millions of books, ought not to be the property only of the scholars and pseudoscholars who use them. There they have dedicated themselves to the strange, incomprehensible, barbaric aim of making these great, these immense libraries accessible not only to scholars, professors and other specialists like them, but to the masses, the crowds, the man in the street.

What a profane use of librarianship! What a lack of that "good order" we take such a justifiable pride in. Instead of rules discussed and elaborated by dozens of official committees, thinking up hundreds of petty restrictions on the use of books, they take care that even children can use rich book collections; they are anxious for readers to read books bought at public expense in their own homes; they see the pride and glory of the public library not in the number of rarities it possesses, not in the sixteenth-century printed books or tenth-century manuscripts, but in the extent to which books circulate among the people, the number of new readers enrolled, the speed with which requests for books are satisfied, the number of books issued for home reading, the number of children enrolled as readers and library users. . . . Strange prejudices are spread abroad in western countries, and it is a cause for rejoicing that in their concern for us our superiors guard us with care and consideration from the influence of these prejudices, shielding our rich public libraries from the mob and the rabble.

Before me lies the report of the New York Public Library for 1911.

In that year the New York Public Library moved from two antiquated buildings to a new one built by the city. The total stock is now about two million volumes. It happened that the first book asked for from the reading room was in Russian. This was a work of N. Grot: *Moral Ideals of Our Time.* The call slip for the book was handed in at 9:08 a.m. The book was delivered to the reader at 9:15 a.m.

During the year 1,658,376 people visited the library, 246,950 readers used the reading room, and 911,891 books were issued. . . .

In 1911 almost eight million—7,914,882—volumes were lent for home reading, four hundred thousand more than in 1910. For each hundred of the population of all ages and both sexes, 267 books were issued for home reading during the year.

Each of the forty-two branch libraries not only provides facilities for consulting reference works on the spot, and for borrowing, but is also a place where evening lectures, public meetings, and cultural entertainments can take place. . . .

For children the New York Public Library has built a special central reading room, and is gradually opening others in the branches. The staff are concerned to provide every facility for children, and supply them with information. Children borrowed a total of 2,859,888 volumes, a little short of three million (and more than a third of the total issue). The number of children visiting the reading room was 1,120,915.

As far as the loss of books is concerned, New York Public Library estimates losses as 70–90 per 100,000 books issued on loan.

This is the position in New York. And in Russia?

—From *Lenin, Krupskaia and Libraries* (Archon Books and Clive Bingley, 1968)

Glimpses These three views of the Carnegie Library of Pittsburgh show a state-of-the-art library in 1912. Here we have the periodical room *(top left)* replete with desks that feature individual lighting, the catalog department *(top right)*, and the main lending desk *(center)*. The larger libraries of the era expressed great pride in the quality of the card catalog. Few would dispute Thomas Carlyle's oft-quoted line of 1849: "A library is not worth anything without a catalogue—it is a Polyphemus without an eye in his head." (CLP)

Harrisburg Built in 1916, this Harrisburg, Pennsylvania, central library is now part of the Dauphin County Library System. At the time it was built there were more than 3,000 public libraries in the nation with holdings of more than a thousand books. (Dauphin County Library System)

Librarian's Office This office as it appeared in 1912 at the Forbes Library in Northampton, Massachusetts. William Parker Cutter, the librarian there until 1911, wrote an occasional column for the local paper called "The Library Alcove." The official history of the library, a fascinating institutional portrait entitled *Disposed to Learn*, contains revealing excerpts from that column including these two:

"The collection of the books in the library, although large, may not contain works wanted by a reader. It is that reader's privilege to have such a book purchased or borrowed, and, with few exceptions, it is the wish of the library to buy it. Many of our people do not, I fear, understand this. The librarian is not a mind reader; he cannot know what is wanted unless told. . . ."

"Some boys playing football last fall on the library grounds broke a window in the library. They have not paid for it. Now, boys, would it not be better to 'fess up' to your father or mother, and get the money together? I fear if you do not you may be disappointed when you want to play there again. Even if you are not, wouldn't you feel better about it? This isn't a threat, understand, just a suggestion. Some time I shall tell you boys about some of the good books you may not have read." (Forbes Library)

COMMANDMENTS AND PROVERBS 1914

TEN COMMANDMENTS FOR BORROWERS OF BOOKS

"Who goeth a-borrowing goeth a-sorrowing"

1. Thou shalt not buy what thou canst borrow.
2. Thou shalt take care of thine own books, for thy babies and thy puppies will find as much delight in borrowed books as playthings.
3. Thou shalt not cut the leaves of a book with a butter-knife, nor decorate the margins with jam in imitation of the old illuminated manuscripts.
4. Remember that the most artistic form of appreciation is to repair the torn leaves of a book with postage-stamp edging, and to arrange the red and green lines alternately.
5. Honor the opinions of an author as expressed in his book, but shouldst thou disagree with his views, pencil thine own notes in the margins. By so doing thou wilt not only give evidence of thy vast learning, but will irritate subsequent readers who will, unmindful of thy superior knowledge, regard thee as a conceited ass.
6. Thou shalt choose thy books from amongst those most worn. Shouldst thou be dissatisfied with their contents thou wilt have the pleasure of knowing that many of thy neighbors have been "had" likewise.
7. Thou shalt consult the librarian when thou knowest not what thou requirest. Should he be unable to assist thee, substitute "in" for "con."
8. Thou shalt not pay fines on principle (current cash is much to be preferred).
9. Thou shalt not bear false witness against the library assistant, saying: "He taketh the best books and reserveth them for his friends."
10. Thou shalt not covet the books that thy neighbor hath appropriated.

PERVERTED PROVERBS

"The price of wisdom is above rubies"

A book in the hand is worth two on the shelf.
It is an ill book that does nobody any good.
Select books in haste and repent at your leisure.
Be slow in choosing a book and slower in reading it.
A book should not be judged by its binding.
Two books are better than one.
Returned in times saves "fine."
Fine books make "fined" borrowers.
A library book is better out than in.
It is easier to criticize a book than to write one.
Better ill-fed than ill-read.
It is a poor book that is not worth the candle.
Many hands make dirty books.
Spare the puppy and spoil the book.
Never buy tomorrow the book you can borrow today.
The reader proposes, the librarian disposes.
It's a long tale that has no ending.

—From *Library Jokes and Jottings,* by Henry T. Coutts (Grafron and Company, 1914)

Mobility They were still called "book wagons" and there were very few of them, but they were beginning to gather some attention. Word of the Washington County motorized unit, shown here *(right)* serving a farm family, was being heard and others began to experiment with them. Plainfield, Indiana, put one on the road in 1916 *(below)*, which made it one of the earliest in the United States. Some years later, Ida Mae Miller, Historic Librarian of Guilford Township Historical Collection, wrote of the debut of the Plainfield vehicle, "A flurry of excitement met the library auto on its first trip, Wednesday, July 26, 1916. Reactions to its appearance were varied. Some thought it an ambulance, medicine wagon, book agent's outfit or popcorn wagon." Circulation from the wagon for the first year was 7,482. (Washington County Free Library and Guilford Township Historical Collection of the Plainfield Public Library)

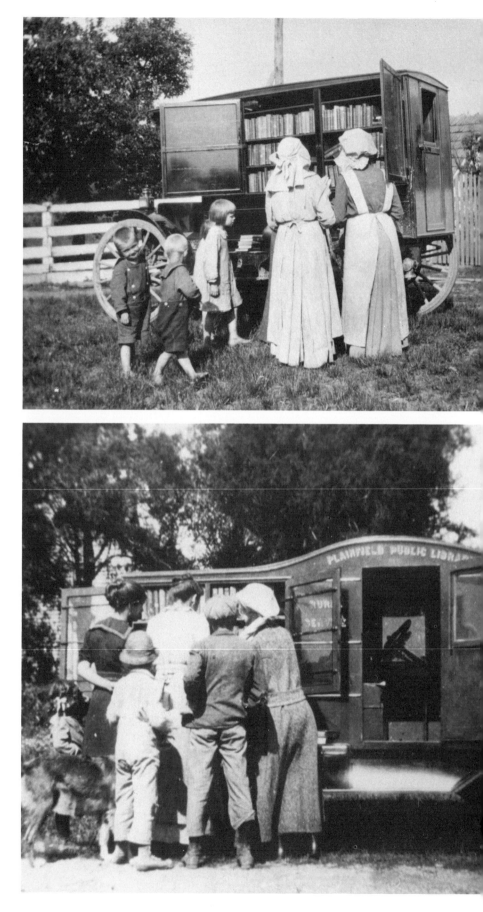

Walk In When Hibbing, Minnesota, put its motorized "library bus" on the road in 1915, another milestone was reached in that it was the first patrons could actually enter. The bus carried a coal stove *(below)* to provide heat when the temperature went below zero. Also shown, the bus making a stop at Carson Lake *(below, right)*, where the population was typically Finnish, Irish, and Serbian, and a view of the bus *(bottom)* with some of its younger clientele. (Hibbing Public Library)

Eve of War A sketch of the St. Louis Public Library *(below)* drawn in 1916 and an undated photograph *(right)* of the Irvington Branch of the Indianapolis Public Library seem illustrative of the days before America was drawn into the Great War. (St. Louis Public Library and the ALA Archives)

Within a few weeks of America's entrance into World War I, the American Library Association was at work on a massive campaign to get reading material into the hands of American forces at home and abroad. The ALA campaign was able to collect $5 million in donations, distribute over ten million books and magazines, and set up thirty-six camp libraries with help from the Carnegie Corporation. In his book on the ALA and World War I, *Books for Sammies*, Arthur P. Young came to this conclusion: "Operating under constraints of limited funds, a small membership (about 3,300 in 1917), and external supervision, the American Library Association's Library War Service program may be judged an unusually successful venture."

Rallying Point In both World Wars the New York Public Library was to become a center for book drives. The general bustle of the area is shown in a 1917 photograph *(top right)* and then we see a book rally on the steps which was held in April 1918. The slogan of the Library War Service, run by the American Library Association, was "a million dollars, for a million books, for a million men." (NYPL and the ALA Library)

THE
ALA
GOES TO WAR
1917–1919

During the war, librarians reaffirmed their belief in the book as a powerful determinant of human intellect and behavior. This faith in the power of print was pervasive: reading produced a contented, efficient army; reading advanced the cause of better citizenship; and reading hastened medical recuperation. Exemplifying this faith, William F. Seward, librarian at Camp Bowie (Texas), confidently proclaimed that "you cannot beat a reading army." Betraying their elitist inclinations, librarians delighted in reporting the cultural works read by soldiers. After the war, libraries were heralded as stabilizing agents in the crusade against radicalism. By condoning the army's censorship of camp library collections, librarians conducted themselves in a manner which they judged was entirely consistent with the belief that reading had a profound influence. The inconsistency of this position would not be confronted for several decades.

Notwithstanding these vestigial attitudes, librarians performed exceptionally well under sometimes exhausting, stressful conditions. Unfamiliar with military customs and without permanent quarters, the first group of camp library organizers impressed the military authorities and the common soldier with their determination to provide a professional service. Never before had librarians been asked to serve such a cross section of the adult population. Having a captive audience (in the camps at least) of grateful soldiers undoubtedly inspired the librarians to extend themselves. Various services and programs, together with such features as accessible collections, testify to the emergence of a more pragmatic, liberal conception of librarianship. Permeating all of these services was the emphasis placed on library extension, the practice of dispersing library collections to as many locations as possible.

The Library War Service was not without imperfections. Competent librarians, especially in Europe, were always in short supply. The excessive loss of books between America and Europe severely reduced the effectiveness of library service in France. Seven million books for 4.5 million soldiers, as John Cotton Dana had bluntly noted, were simply inadequate. In spite of the Association's best efforts, many soldiers never got close to an ALA book. Certainly, female librarians did not receive an equitable share of the administrative positions in the camps, and the Association sometimes experienced an estranged relationship with the YMCA.

The Library War Service episode had immediate and long-term consequences. As the greatest mass demonstration of military library service in history, the Library War Service program was particularly successful in the short term. Librarians were proud of their contribution to the war effort, soldiers appreciated library facilities away from home, and military departments assimilated the ALA programs following the Armistice. Similarly, the hospital library service continued, first under the U.S. Public Health Service and then under the sponsorship of the Veteran's Bureau. Creation of the American Merchant Marine Library Association and the American Library in Paris were permanent legacies. The successful financial campaigns and the widespread approbation of its wartime services were heady experiences for an obscure professional association.

—From *Books for Sammies*, by Arthur P. Young (Beta Phi Mu, 1981)

Reminder Bookplate placed in the books distributed by the American Library Association. The smiling doughboy with his towering pile of books was used widely and can be seen in the large poster in front of the New York Public Library in the last picture. (Smithsonian)

WAR SERVICE LIBRARY

·THIS·BOOK·IS PROVIDED·BY THE·PEOPLE OF·THE UNITED·STATES THROUGH·THE AMERICAN LIBRARY ASSOCIATION FOR THE·USE·OF THE·SOLDIERS AND·SAILORS

Soldier Reading "I found your books everywhere," wrote a returning American official to Herbert Putnam, who headed the ALA book drive as Librarian of Congress, "from the seaport bases to the front line trenches. I found them in dugouts thirty to forty feet below the ground, in cow-barns where the shrapnel had blown part of the roof away, as well as in substantial huts and tents far back from the firing line. And they were well worn books that I saw, showing signs of constant usage. Indeed, the books are in continual demand. I am sure that it will be a reading army that we will welcome home. . . ." (ALA Archives)

Camp Libraries The extent of ALA activity can been seen in these views of camp libraries (Camp Beauregard, Louisiana, *above*, Camp Wadsworth, South Carolina, *right*, and Camp Dodge, Iowa, *opposite, top*) and military hospital service (at Camp Wadsworth, *opposite center*, and Camp Meade in Maryland, *opposite bottom*) The hospital scenes appear on postcards with an appeal for magazines for the men in hospitals. (ALA Archives and Author's collection)

CAMP LIBRARY, AMERICAN LIBRARY ASSOCIATION, CAMP WADSWORTH, SOUTH CAROLINA

CAMP LIBRARY, AMERICAN LIBRARY ASSOCIATION,
CAMP DODGE, IOWA

*Library Service of the
American Library As-
sociation in the Base
Hospital, Camp Wads-
worth, S.C.*

*Reading in the Red
Cross House. The
A. L. A. has placed
libraries in 208 hos-
pitals.*

*The men in hospitals and
camps here and overseas
need your magazines. As
soon as you have read
them, place a stamp on
the notice on the cover,
and mail.*

*Bedside service of the
American Library Asso-
ciation in the Base Hos-
pital, Camp Meade, Md.*

*With her book truck,
the librarian brings to
the man's bed the book
he wants. The A.L.A.
has placed libraries in
208 hospitals.*

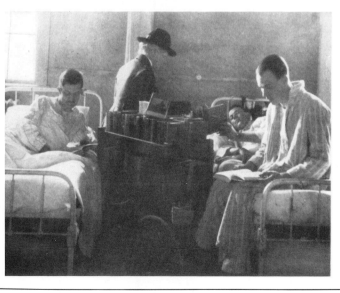

*The men in hospitals and
camps here and overseas
need your magazines. As
soon as you have read
them, place a stamp on
the notice on the cover,
and mail.*

77

THE TWENTIES BRANCHING OUT IN ALL DIRECTIONS

This was a period of continued momentum. Andrew Carnegie had passed away in 1919, but the grants kept coming through the offices of the Carnegie Corporation. Bookmobiles were coming into their own and were being put on the road in all shapes, sizes, and configurations. Inspired and instructed by the military hospital work of World War I and its aftermath, hospital ward service was becoming part of the varied and growing package of special services offered by many libraries.

THREE

Urban Landmarks The 1920s saw the completion of some of the nation's most stunning central city libraries—many of which still stand in their original glory. Among them:

Los Angeles Dedicated in 1926, this great downtown library building *(right)* mixes the Art Deco and International styles. Already the largest institution of its kind west of Chicago, it was just beginning a major expansion that would have doubled its size when it was devastated by an arsonist's fire. (Los Angeles Public Library)

Philadelphia This Central Building on Benjamin Franklin Parkway *(overleaf top)* opened to the public in 1927. The block-long structure, which still stands as one of the largest American public libraries, is a replica of the eighteenth-century French revival Ministry of Marine building in Paris. (Free Library of Philadelphia)

Detroit The Main Library *(overleaf bottom)* was dedicated in 1921. It was rededicated in 1963 after a major expansion. Ironically, the original building had been designed to serve the city for at least 50 years, but it had become apparent only a few years after it opened that it would soon be outgrown. The Library's 1925–26 annual report pointed out, "The Present Main Library originally designed for a city which MIGHT grow to a million population is now serving a city well beyond that mark." (Detroit Public Library)

Urban Wheels A pioneer in the use of the bookmobile within city limits, Evanston, Illinois, launched its first on June 21, 1920. The Evanston *News-Index* of June 12, 1920, pointed out, "Evanston is to be the first city in Illinois and one of the first municipalities in the country to serve people in the outlying districts with books by means of a branch library conducted on an auto truck." (Library Journal collection)

Book Coupes Ingenuity was the order of the day as the concept of the mobile branch took hold and some cities and counties simply took production-line automobiles and modified them to hold a few shelves of books. Two examples from Indiana: a Ford Coupe *(above)* in the service of the Public Library of Fort Wayne and Allen County and another *(right)* from Vanderburgh County. (ALA Library and *Library Journal*)

WHEN LIBRARIES TAKE TO THE OPEN ROAD 1926

The perambulating "book bus" has indefinitely extended the radius of the circulating library. A wholly new class of readers in the smaller towns and villages today is regularly served by these vehicles, which often venture far afield to visit remote farms, ranches and mining camps. Although the automobile library is but two years old, it has had a surprising development and is now in active operation in practically every State.

The traveling library makes possible an entirely new application of the open shelf practice. Even when traveling at high speed along country roads it has considerable educational value. The well-ordered book shelves behind their glass doors bring a suggestion of urban culture to the villages along the route and to the laborer in the fields. Arrived at a crossroad or a lonely farmhouse, the doors are thrown open and an attractive library is available miles from the ordinary base of supplies.

The librarian who pilots the book bus and presides over its shelves must be extremely versatile. The work is usually entrusted to a young lady who combines general culture and special library training with a working knowledge of the machinery of the automobile. She must enter sympathetically into the lives of her clients and understand their needs and at the same time be able to meet the local officials and tactfully handle many difficult problems. She is often dressed in knickerbockers, for the library must often make its rounds in all extremes of weather. In the more important systems someone is usually found to run the car, and the library goes afield with a crew of two. . . .

It is not uncommon for one of these perambulating libraries to travel upward of 100 miles in a single day, although the average is lower. To cover fifty miles, with some eight stops for distributing and collecting books, is considered an excellent day's work. The libraries follow prescribed routes, making calls at fixed points on a regular schedule. They are thus available on certain days and hours at the public schools, at definite points in towns and villages, before the local post office or at crossroads along the route. By following a regular time table the library usually arrives to find a group of clients awaiting it, bringing the books left the week before, so that an exchange may be made with little loss of time. . . .

The life of the book-bus librarian often demands downright hard work and physical endurance. They are sometimes obliged to make more than a day's run, and it frequently happens that the librarians must live the life of a pioneer. Mrs. May Dexter Henshall, a well-known librarian of California, writes for instance:

> I have known the joys of the best hotels and the sorrows of the worst. Sleeping on a hay stack in a barn was not the most appalling.

The perambulating librarian finds her rewards in carrying the right books to those who have been denied them. An old gentleman was found in the mountains of California far from a railroad, who has been longing for years to read Morley's *Life of Gladstone*. Ten years before he had read a review of the book, but had never had the opportunity to purchase or borrow it. He had slowly saved a part of the price of the book when the traveling library penetrated to his home.

—From the *New York Times Book Review*, January 10, 1926, by Francis A. Collins

The zeal and idealism that accompanied the burgeoning bookmobile movement was considerable. "The automobile and the good roads," said a California librarian to the *New York Times*, "are throwing a magic bridge over the slough of despond which once lay between the old farmstead and the town. And the library by bringing books to the rancher's door makes farming a surer undertaking and country life a fuller joy."

Books on Wheels In the 1920s many libraries initiated bookmobile service, and some graphic evidence of those times remains: outside *(above right)* and inside *(above)* a vehicle that was the pride of Ramsey County, Minnesota; a motorized branch of the Monmouth County, N.J., Library *(right)* serves readers of all ages; and a truck named "The Cardinal" *(opposite bottom)* serves the children of a one-teacher school in Dauphin County, Pennsylvania. Two other pictures survive with no location noted but they show the popular side-opening style of the period. The original caption of the boy climbing up to get his books *(opposite top left)* reads: "He knows what he wants and gets it." (U.S. Office of Education)

Book Drop The usefulness of motorized vehicles was not restricted to bookmobiles. Here a Washington, D.C., library truck is used to deliver books to a public school. (Office of Education)

On the Wards In hundreds of communities, libraries were purchasing wheeled carts for hospital service. Carts are shown here from the Sioux City, Iowa, Public Library *(right)* and the Minneapolis Public Library *(bottom)*. Not until the advent of hospital television would the importance of this library service be eclipsed. (*Library Journal* and Minneapolis Public Library)

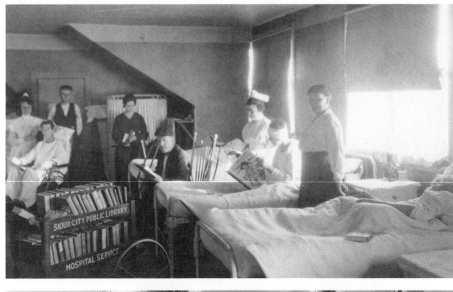

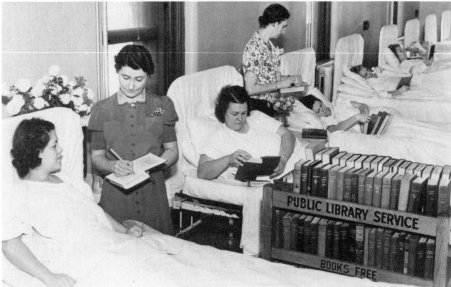

EPISODE IN THE ADVENTURES OF A LIBRARIAN 1920s

IN SEARCH OF A FATHER'S HEART

In our Library all barriers between the people and the Librarian have long since been removed. Children are not confined to the Children's Room; my office door is always as wide open as was Tom Marshall's at the Capitol, and I am always pleased when the silent invitation of the open door is accepted.

Nevertheless, I confess that one day, as I felt the swift approach of a tall stranger, saw his eager eyes fixed upon me, and heard his impetuous question, "Have you got my Father's heart?" my hand involuntarily started toward the telephone that connects with the Police station, and I breathed a silent prayer that it might be in working order.

My visitor, however, immediately showed me that, crazy as he might seem, he still retained a sense of propriety. He withdrew a step or two, and stood quietly but earnestly looking at me, as if he really expected an answer to his astonishing question. So still holding the telephone unlifted, I replied:

"No, I have not your Father's heart: has he lost it?"

"It's this way," he explained. "More than forty years ago my Father, on his way from Albany to Boston, stopped over for a day in Pittsfield. As he was crossing your North Street, he fell dead. No one knew him and, after a few fruitless inquiries, his body was sent to your Berkshire Medical College, where an autopsy showed that his death was due to an unusual lesion of the heart. The 'case,' indeed, proved so interesting to the examiner that, after the body was properly buried, the heart was preserved in alcohol to illustrate future lectures. When I first heard of this, I was rather shocked; but we all at home accepted it as a fact and did nothing about it. As time went on, however, and especially after the death of my mother, the idea of Father's heart being in a glass bottle in the hands of strange men in a distant town became increasingly painful, and at last so intolerable that I have made a long journey, to see whether I can recover the missing part of my Father's body, and give it decent interment in our family lot. This morning I was told that the Medical College was burned down several years ago, but that the scientific books and apparatus and pathological specimens had been saved and presented to your Library and Museum. If this is true, let me ask again whether it may not be possible that we may find the heart somewhere in the old collection?"

I gave him the right hand of sympathy, and told him that all the specimens of the old College had been transferred to our city hospital.

He thanked me, and departed to continue what I fear is a fruitless quest. I do not know what truth there may have been in his tale; but, in his right mind or out of it, I am sure that he is sincere and sad—and harmless. I record the adventure so that none of my readers may be unduly alarmed if he should some day hear from an excited stranger's lips the startling question: "Have you got my Father's heart?"

—From *Adventures of a Librarian,* by Harlan H. Ballard (Walter Neale, 1929)

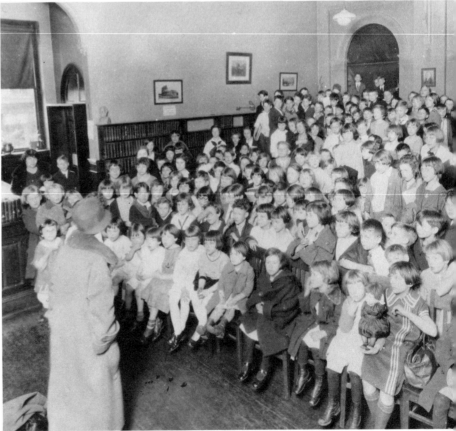

Children's Hours If children had been excluded or just barely tolerated as nineteenth-century patrons, they had become prime clients of the public libraries in the 1920s, and their business was eagerly sought. Children's Book Week 1922 is promoted in the window of the Fox Film Corp. *(opposite top)* with a cinematic tie-in and a story hour at one of the Enoch Pratt Free Library branches *(opposite bottom)* in Baltimore. (ALA Library and Enoch Pratt Free Library)

Doll Reception Early each year the girls of Northampton, Massachusetts, were invited to bring their dolls (especially those they had just gotten for Christmas) to the Forbes Library to meet the dolls in the collection housed there. These images are from a reception held in the 1920s and reflect the urge to make children a vital part of library life. (Forbes Library)

Points of Local Pride A selection of postcards shows the variety of small-town libraries before the Depression. Despite claims to the contrary, they were not all neoclassical in design but came in a variety of shapes and sizes. Exteriors shown *(right)* are from Buena Park, California; Charlestown, New Hampshire; Brandon, Vermont; and *(opposite)* Ashland, Oregon; Bernardsville, New Jersey; and North Anson, Maine. Writing about such libraries in his book *The American Small Town*, John A. Jakle typified such places: "The town library was a storehouse of knowledge, a ready place of reference. It was also a place of entertainment, for reading was a primary source of relaxation before the age of radio and television. The library was female dominated. The librarian was usually a dedicated but underpaid woman. Most patrons were married women, although their visits might serve the reading habits of husbands and children as well. The library was the only place in town where one could venture regularly in search of both change of scene and intellectual stimulation. It was an interface with the outside world of ideas." (Author's collection)

Public Library, Bernardsville, N. J.

Stewart Public Library, N. Anson, Me. 42

Beyond the Portals Most smaller libraries featured a children's room or section, a reading room with huge wooden tables, and an uplifting piece of sculpture. Here we see the children's room at the St. Johnsbury, Vermont, Atheneum Free Public Library. *(right)* Also shown *(center)* is the reading room at the Gordon Nash Library in New Hampton, New Hampshire, and *(below)* the Rockland, Maine, Public Library. (Author's collection)

CHILDREN'S ROOM · IN THE DAVID A. HOWE PUBLIC LIBRARY, WELLSVILLE, NEW YORK.

Published by F. W. Sanborn & Co.   Interior of Gordon Nash Library, New Hampton, N. H.

SPECIAL COLLECTIONS: A CASE IN POINT 1928

[John G.] White was the greatest benefactor the Cleveland Public Library has ever had. From 1884, when he was elected to its board for the first time, until his death in 1928 the library was foremost in his thoughts. He was responsible for the great White Collection of Orientalia, Folklore, and Chess, which has fully justified the inclusion of his name in the list of American book collectors, along with the Huntingtons, Folgers, Morgans, and Newberrys. . . .

White believed strongly that every man should have hobbies. In his younger days he had taken a great interest in yachting, to the point where he was able to design and build his own craft; at that time he had cruised the Great Lakes in his cabin yacht *Camilla*. In this case he thought the hobby also gave him certain advantages in his profession; he learned enough to understand and handle admiralty and maritime cases at law. After that, he developed a fascination for old maps and began to collect them as a means of studying world conditions and historic changes. Soon he came to the conclusion that chess was more educational, with the result that his collection on chess and checkers, still by far the largest in the world, was on its way. White was himself an able chess player in his early years. In the 1880s he played a series with the current world's champion; he lost more games than he won, but his performance was a creditable one.

White's collection of chess memorabilia was all-inclusive. For printed books his aim was to buy every edition of every book and as many manuscripts as possible—ultimately nearly one thousand manuscripts. One of the latter, purchased by White in 1909, was published in 1480 and contained Jean de Vignay's translation of a manuscript by Jacobus de Cessolis, *De ludo scacchorum* ("On the Game of Chess"). Sometimes there are collateral benefits from such purchases, and there was with this acquisition. The Cessolis manuscript happened to be bound with several political treatises in Latin, one of which was *Oculis pastoralis pascens officia*. This later turned out to be unique and famous and is now known among Italian scholars as *Il Codice de Cleveland.*

In addition to the materials primarily concerned with chess, White collected important literary works that make significant reference to the game. Castiglione's *The Courtier*, a well-known treatise on etiquette, social problems, and intellectual accomplishments which was published in 1518, is represented in the White Collection by 57 editions from the sixteenth century alone. The *Gesta Romanorum*, actually a collection of medieval Latin stories that has little to do with Roman history, is found in the chess collection in 46 editions, including 9 printed in the fifteenth century. There is the *Rubaiyat of Omar Khayyam* in the priceless Fitzgerald edition of 1859. Another valuable by-product of White's interest is the collection of Rabelais. Because Rabelais wrote of chess, White brought together as complete a collection of editions of *Gargantua and Pantagruel* as exists anywhere; there are at least 120 editions comprising 304 volumes.

When White died in 1928 he gave the Cleveland Public Library all of his Chess and Checkers Collection, which he had retained in his possession during his lifetime. . . .

—From *Open Shelves and Open Minds*, by C. H. Cramer (Case Western University Press, 1972)

More Deposits Though branch libraries were growing in number in the 1920s, deposit-station libraries were still a popular way to get books to people. This 1926 photograph shows one of them at a fire station in Northampton, Massachusetts. (Forbes Library)

Beyond Books Increasingly the public library was being seen as a place to house and display more than the printed word. Collections of all sorts were being accepted and one could walk into a library and encounter a case of extinct birds, a display devoted to Victorian toys, a chess match in progress, or a small collection of live animals. Shown here is Grace Wiley with two members of the reptile menagerie—a gila monster and a rattlesnake—at the Minneapolis Public Library. The collection was featured at the library from 1922 to 1933. Wiley was bitten by one of her charges in 1928 and was hospitalized for several days. In 1948 Wiley was doing reptile research in California and was posing one of her cobras in the open-hooded attack position for a *Time* photographer when she was bitten on the finger. She died ninety minutes later. (Minneapolis Public Library)

Restaurant Library This photograph of a library in a restaurant with a bookmobile in front carried the original caption, "Spot the sign 'County Library Free Service.' This is in a restaurant on a bridge over Five Mile Creek, Brookside. This community is the most European in atmosphere of any of our communities." The town is just north of Birmingham, Alabama. *(Library Journal)*

Segregated Branch This image lacks a date and is simply marked "Colored Branch, Tampa." Placing it in the 1920s is based on a guess, but the date is not important because it so vividly displays the fact that segregation was very much a part of American public-library history. Ironically, Tampa was probably proud of the progress represented by this picture as other places simply prohibited all blacks from the library, save for when they were returning or picking up books for white patrons. *(Library Journal)*

HOW A BLACK MAN GOT BOOKS FROM THE MEMPHIS LIBRARY LATE 1920s

[One morning Richard Wright picked up the local Memphis paper and came upon an editorial which was a "furious denunciation" of H. L. Mencken. Wright wanted to know more about this man who was able to call down the "scorn of the South." There was a large library in the city, but it was only for whites. Wright had been there but only to get books for white men. He was determined to read Mencken and had to be very careful about picking one of the white men he worked with to help him trick the library into letting a black man borrow a book.]

There remained only one man whose attitude did not fit into an anti-Negro category, for I had heard the white men refer to him as a "Pope lover." He was an Irish Catholic and was hated by the white southerners. I knew that he read books, because I had got him volumes from the library several times. Since he, too, was an object of hatred, I felt that he might refuse me but would hardly betray me. I hesitated, weighing and balancing the imponderable realities.

One morning I paused before the Catholic fellow's desk.

"I want to ask you a favor," I whispered to him.

"What is it?"

"I want to read. I can't get books from the library. I wonder if you'd let me use your card?"

He looked at me suspiciously.

"My card is full most of the time," he said.

"I see," I said and waited, posing my question silently.

"You're not trying to get me into trouble, are you, boy?" he asked, staring at me.

"Oh, no, sir."

"What book do you want?"

"A book by H. L. Mencken."

"Which one?"

"I don't know. Has he written more than one?"

"He has written several."

"I didn't know that."

"What makes you want to read Mencken?"

"Oh, I just saw his name in the newspaper," I said.

"It's good of you to want to read," he said. "But you ought to read the right things."

I said nothing. Would he want to supervise my reading?

"Let me think," he said. "I'll figure out something."

I turned from him and he called me back. He stared at me quizzically.

"Richard, don't mention this to the other white men," he said.

"I understand," I said. "I won't say a word."

A few days later he called me to him.

"I've got a card in my wife's name," he said. "Here's mine."

"Thank you, sir."

"Do you think you can manage it?"

"I'll manage fine," I said.

"If they suspect you, you'll get in trouble," he said.

"I'll write the same kind of notes to the library that you wrote when you sent me for books," I told him. "I'll sign your name."

He laughed.

"Go ahead. Let me see what you get," he said.

That afternoon I addressed myself to forging a note. Now, what were the names of books written by H. L. Mencken? I did not know any of them. I finally wrote what I thought would be a foolproof note: *Dear Madam: Will you please let this nigger boy*—I used the word "nigger" to make the librarian feel that I could not possibly be the author of the note—*have some books by H. L. Mencken?* I forged the white man's name.

I entered the library as I had always done when on errands for whites, but I felt that I would somehow slip up and betray myself. I doffed my hat, stood a respectful distance from the desk, looked as unbookish as possible, and waited for the white patrons to be taken care of. When the desk was clear of people, I still waited. The white librarian looked at me.

"What do you want, boy?"

As though I did not possess the power of speech, I stepped forward and simply handed her the forged note, not parting my lips.

"What books by Mencken does he want?" she asked.

"I don't know, ma'am," I said, avoiding her eyes.

"Who gave you this card?"

"Mr. Falk," I said.

"Where is he?"

"He's at work, at the M—— Optical Company," I said. "I've been in here for him before."

"I remember," the woman said. "But he never wrote notes like this."

Oh, God, she's suspicious. Perhaps she would not let me have the books? If she had turned her back at that moment, I would have ducked out the door and never gone back. Then I thought of a bold idea.

"You can call him up, ma'am," I said, my heart pounding.

"You're not using these books, are you?" she asked pointedly.

"Oh, no, ma'am. I can't read."

"I don't know what he wants by Mencken," she said under her breath.

I knew now that I had won; she was thinking of other things and the race question had gone out of her mind. She went to the shelves. Once or twice she looked over her shoulder at me, as though she was still doubtful. Finally she came forward with two books in her hand.

"I'm sending him two books," she said. "But tell Mr. Falk to come in next time, or send me the names of the books he wants. I don't know what he wants to read."

—From *Black Boy*, by Richard Wright (Harper, 1945)

THE THIRTIES
BREAD LINES
OF THE SPIRIT

"Yes! We have gas! Yes! We have lights! Yes! We have a LIBRARY!" read a 1930 ad from a real-estate development company that was creating the Garden Villas Community outside of Houston. The library was the developer's field office, which had been filled with shelves and books. The ad reflected the importance of the public library in hard times and the continuing drive to offer some form of library service to everyone in the country. Despite the Great Depression, by 1935 about 63 percent of the population was served by a free public library.

If it was a time of declining book budgets and salary cuts, it was also a time for sharply increased circulation. The library had become a relief agency of its own—"the bread line

FOUR

of the spirit" was a common description—and great efforts were made to keep them open and operating. In Cleveland, the library actually found itself sponsoring "Overdue Weeks," in which patrons who could afford it were asked to keep books beyond their due date so that fines could be levied at the rate of 12 cents a book per week. The New Deal in the form of the Work Progress Administration was to have a profound impact on library life in America. If critics of the WPA wanted to call it a make-work agency whose initials really stood for "We-Putter-Around," they had a hard time making those charges stick when it came to library work.

The library works performed under the Work Progress Administration (1934–1943) were many and varied. Buildings were built and repaired, catalogs and indexes prepared, delapidated books repaired, and demonstration units set up in many local areas. By the end of 1940 the library projects of the WPA employed more than 27,000 people and involved annual expenditures of over $18 million in federal funds.

Fortunately, this New Deal agency was careful to document its work, and today some 121,610 images of the WPA and its predecessor agencies are housed at the National Archives. Within that collection are more than a thousand relating to public libraries, from which this sampling was made.

Pack Horse Librarians One of the most innovative WPA programs was based in Kentucky, where carriers, mostly women, mounted horses and mules to go to remote sections of the state to serve mountain folks with books. They would meet once a week at their headquarters to replenish their saddlebags. Shown here are: mounted carriers at their headquarters in Knott County *(below)*; a librarian making a call at a mountain school *(right)*; a lone librarian on her mule in the Cut Shin Creek area of Leslie County *(opposite top)*; a patron reading a copy of *Good Housekeeping*, which had been brought to her cabin in Mill Creek, by pack horse *(opposite, lower left)*; and an elderly woman *(opposite, lower right)* reading a book that had been brought home by her niece from a school served by pack horse. (National Archives, all photos taken by the WPA in 1938)

101

THE WPA COMES TO MINNEAPOLIS 1930s

When the throes of economic depression forced Minneapolis' many cultural institutions to reckon with everyday existence, the prospect of WPA assistance was a welcome sight to Librarian Gratia Countryman. She retired in 1936 after 32 years as the head of a major facility, but not before planning and implementing the beginning of WPA library aid in 1935. Though much has been written about the library's many accomplishments, due attention and analysis have not been given to that historical chapter involving federal patronage. To a Library Board faced with diminished services, the prospect of federal assistance was more than welcome. At the library, there was none of the political challenge or professional reticence that characterized many of the WPA's cultural projects around the country. The WPA meant carpenters who could build new cases for display, and the utilization of staff to unpack, clean, sort, remount, reclassify, and recondition the major attractions. To this cause, however, Gratia Countryman saw something more, and her own creative yet practical stamp is seen on the four major projects that were undertaken, the first in September, 1935.

The American Thirties produced a turning-in in many communities, a desire to look around and become better acquainted with its regional environment and historical roots. Nowhere was this condition more evident than in the library's various WPA efforts that were undertaken "to extend the facilities of the Minneapolis Public Library." Indeed, the common thread throughout all of the programs is that of community awareness and the recognition of specific community needs that the Library might be able to serve.

CLASSES AND FORUMS

The Minneapolis Public Library developed a large number of free classes and forums for various constituencies which were based on community need or interest. A number of forums and classes emphasized healthful living and personal health with the kind of application that would have the broadest appeal. A strong effort was made to raise the consciousness of the community on health concerns. . . .

THE NEEDS OF THE UNEMPLOYED

In a direct response to a major community need—personal assistance for citizens caught up in economic and psychological difficulty—the WPA made it possible to provide needed counseling and job guidance. High unemployment in the Twin Cities area called for specific responses, and it was a credit to the library's Vocational Adjustment Clinic that many individuals were brought through the anxieties of a very trying period with professional assistance. As an outgrowth of the job counseling project, a number of discussion groups were formed to concentrate on personal needs. The results of this extension of service emphasized the increased self-awareness, worth and dignity of the "unemployed" participants. The counseling program made it clear that certain projects had the capacity to be successful in the community functions the library assumed. That the Minneapolis Public Library could become a moving social force in dealing with personal problems was a major departure from the image of a building that simply held books. . . .

—From *Studies in Creative Partnership,* edited by Daniel F. Ring, from the section by John Franklin White (Scarecrow Press, 1980)

Books on the Bayou In this scene from Issaquena, Mississippi, a WPA worker delivers books to tenant-farm families from her bayou boat route. (National Archives)

Minnesota Demonstration In an effort to get library books into small towns, WPA projects were funded to set up "stations" in places ranging from firehouses to barbershops. Here is a cluster of photos showing a few of many stations in the ambitious Minnesota Demonstration Project. These are Lester Frost's Barber Shop in Hollandale *(below left)*, the porch of a farmhouse in Freeborn County (where the books are shelved in orange crates; *below right*), Lars Kvalo's General Store in Freeborn County *(overleaf lower left)*, the office of the Rayeslucas Lumber Company in Waltham *(overleaf top)*, and at Lloyd's Lunch, home of the Hartland Book Station *(overleaf, lower right; National Archives, photos taken by the WPA in 1939 and 1940)*

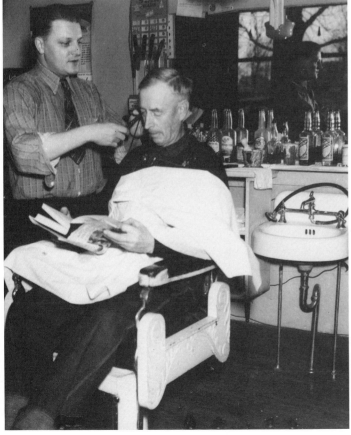

WPA on Wheels An important element of the WPA effort to boost public libraries was to sponsor bookmobiles. Here we see bookmobiles in rural Connecticut *(above)* and at a Farm Security Administration Defense Housing Project near the Hercules Powder Plant in Radford, Virginia *(right)*, and an odd vehicle called the "Travelog"—a log cabin on wheels—serving rural parts of North Carolina *(overleaf top)*. The "Travelog" served three counties where there had been no library service of any kind. In its first four months of operation, it distributed more than 5,000 books. (National Archives)

New Territory Part of the idealism of the WPA library program was to get books and librarians into places where they had not been before. Demonstration projects were set up in places as diverse as prisons, mental hospitals, and military bases. Shown is graphic evidence from the Riker's Island, New York, prison *(below)*, where traveling WPA librarians visited each cell block twice each week; from the Delaware State Hospital for the Insane in Wilmington *(right top)*, where a WPA worker is shown assisting in the library; and from a New Jersey depot *(right bottom)*, where WPA librarians are collecting and arranging books to be sent to soldiers stationed at Fort Dix. (National Archives)

Patrons The WPA carefully documented the fact that its many programs were actually getting its books into the hands of readers. A ferryboat operator, a miner, and a log-cabin dweller are examples from the rich collection of patron images from that time. The original description from the back of the photo of the man in the log cabin: "Creed Hanson enjoys a book borrowed from the branch library maintained by the WPA in Gallia in Gallia County, Ohio, a mile from his home which is a log cabin." (National Archives)

Great Hall Not all library efforts of the 1930s were measured in terms of austerity. This is the main hall *(opposite)* of the Folger Shakespeare Library in Washington at the time the library was dedicated on April 23, 1932, on the 268th anniversary of the Bard's birth. The library was built to house the internationally famous collection of Henry C. Folger. (Underwood and Underwood photo in the Author's collection)

Innovation In this WPA Wilderness Library in Jasper, Arkansas *(right)*, a magazine rack is fashioned from a ladder. (National Archives)

Shanty This library *(below)*, housed in a work shanty, was established by the WPA for WPA workers in Indiana. It was staffed by a WPA librarian and boasted a collection of between 3,000 and 4,000 books. (National Archives)

The Pratt When it opened in 1933, the new main branch of the Enoch Pratt Free Library in Baltimore was seen as a departure in that some of its major design inspiration came from the modern department store. The building *(above right)* came right up to the sidewalk and featured a dozen large windows for display. Inside, an "open plan" was in effect. The voters had approved the city taking a loan of $3 million to add this handsome building to the Enoch Pratt system. In 1882, Pratt, a New Englander who had made his fortune in Baltimore, gave the city a central library, four branches (one for each corner of the city), and an endowment. The total value of the gift was $1,145,833. When the buildings were dedicated in 1886, Pratt said they were to be made available to all, "rich and poor without distinction of race or color." Shown here is the new building as it looked in 1933 and a later view *(below opposite)* of a second-floor reading area. (Enoch Pratt Free Library)

Grand Portal The immense main entrance *(upper right opposite)* to the new Enoch Pratt Free Library seemed to reflect the desire of libraries of the era to encourage the walk-in trade. It is shown here just before its 1933 opening. (Enoch Pratt Free Library)

112

ENOCH PRATT
FREE LIBRARY

LIBRARY ST. MARY'S COLLEGE

Urban Undertaking The WPA made a point of helping and publicizing its efforts to help libraries serving black and integrated communities. Shown here are two WPA-assisted libraries: one *(below)* in a "negro section," as the 1930s caption has it, of Seattle and another *(right)* in the Urban League Branch of the Warren, Ohio, Public Library. (National Archives)

A WEEK IN THE LIFE OF A BOOK BUS, HIBBING, MINNESOTA

Monday night: 6:30 to 9:00 in winter, returning earlier in summer. At Webb they are eager for late fiction, Western and mystery stories; the Seaman's are most in demand. At Morris there must always be outdoor magazines, travel books, all the Halliburtons including *New Worlds to Conquer,* magazines, and World War stories for the head of the house.

Tuesday: 9–11 A.M. Visit to the Pool School—two rooms—first and second grades. The pupils of one room rush to the Bus, followed by the teacher, who helps to fit them out with easy reading books—a novel or two and several periodicals for herself. One Tuesday in three weeks in the afternoon the Wagon goes south on Star Route, where they carry their books in baskets—one family will often take two dozen at a time. At two of these stops music periodicals are in demand. Mitchell School next, here they besiege the Bus by the time it stops. There is no small group that demands as great variety. Then to Kitzville, largely Italian and Slovenian. Stop is made here until after school buses arrive. Then to Albany—on alternate weeks—almost all French who take armloads of English books. Then again to Mitchell.

Wednesday: Half day for work in the library.

Thursday afternoon: Three locations, Mahoning, making six stops, including a two-room school, waiting here for buses bringing high school students. Utica next. Many of the children get books for their parents, big brothers and sisters. Then Kerr, where the auburn-haired "twins" get loads of magazines for mother, always watching for any new stories for girls, and occasionally a book in French. After the school bus has come the trip is concluded by going to the Great Northern Power Plant, returning about 5 in winter, or 4:30 in warm weather. Evening: 6–9 in winter, 6–8 when warmer. Another mining location, Stevenson, one section Italian, another Finnish.

Friday: Three distinct country all-day trips, each in a different direction, which vary from sixteen to twenty-three miles out, stopping both at farm homes and schools and including many more homes in summer as the pupils in winter take books not only for themselves but the rest of the family.

Saturday, 9–12:30 or later. Nelson—Slovenian community. Kelly Lake. A regular, a man who has lost his left hand, lives in an auto home of his own—a square collapsible tent mounted on the truck, which has within it every convenience—and a radio. He works for one of the mining companies for the six or seven months, then for southern lands with its fishing and hunting. Leetonia—Finnish and Croatian—with Louis Stone, "who had read everything"—but must be supplied with new books for boys. Morton—Croatian—a location with more boy patrons than any other.

The work has a charm all its own. One may come in dead tired, dirty, late for dinner, but what matter, if the day has been a happy one, if not, tomorrow is another day. Its informality opens a long, wide road of opportunity.

—From *Library Journal,* September 1, 1930, "The Book Bus in the Arrowhead," by Ada Florence Fitch

Depression-Era Bookmobiles With or without the aid of the WPA, the 1930s saw bookmobiles of all types on the American road. The first vehicle *(right)* is from the Tri-Parish Library in Louisiana, which began in 1937 under the sponsorship of the Louisiana Library Association, whose *Bulletin* pointed out at the time, "It was on June 12 that the tri-parish library began its services to the 30,000 or more white residents of the three parishes chosen for this unique demonstration." Also shown are examples from Cleveland *(below)*, North Carolina *(below opposite)*, and Denver *(opposite top)*. The Denver book trailer was an early example of a walk-through vehicle, even though the first of its kind had appeared in Hibbing, Minnesota, in 1915. (Office of Education, ALA Archives, and Denver Public Library)

116

FACING
ARMAGEDDON
1935–1939

In the second half of the decade, the ideology of uncompromising freedom passed from outsiders, dissidents, and idealistic neophytes to the professional library leaders. This movement occurred when the value of democracy, challenged from abroad and assailed from within, was embraced with increasing fervor. Yet these factors do not alone explain the adoption of the 1939 Library Bill of Rights. To them must be added pressure from a segment of the profession upon its leaders. . . .

Demands for loyalty oaths and other challenges made academic freedom an issue in universities and schools and a major dispute at the 1935 National Education Association conference. . . . James T. Farrell's *A World I Never Made* was tried for obscenity and acquitted. Uniting against fascism, liberals and Communists joined forces in the Popular Front.

A mood of self-questioning swept the professions. Even federal officials questioned the notion of the technically competent, neutral expert, detached from social responsibility. In totalitarian countries, asked Oscar Chapman, Secretary of the Interior, had professionals—librarians, students, writers, research people—"so lost themselves in their own fields of service that they failed to understand the social forces preparing to destroy their work?" He urged professionals to turn from technical problems to help solve the social and economic problems of their time; librarians in particular could bridge the gap between experts and the public. John Studebaker, U.S. Secretary of Education, linked his public forums to a critique of intellectuals and elites: "We can no longer depend upon the understanding of college and university graduates, trickling down to the masses of American citizens."

From a more radical perspective, professional leaders were accused of betrayal. An anonymous young librarian, "Jay Otis," charged that the library profession was dominated by executives whose philosophy and interests were closely linked to those of the business world and who deplored the "overproduction" of librarians when four-tenths of the people lacked library service. Publicists puffed the library "as a social safety valve serving to drain off militancy and any desire to struggle collectively for better immediate conditions and a better social order." Library executives sabotaged libraries and culture with their ruthless economies and "secret censorship":

> Libraries seldom admit that they practice censorship. When hard pressed, they call it "a proper choice of books with a limited book fund." Anything not in keeping with the ideas of the library board (which is usually composed of business and "professional" men and almost never includes a "working man") is ruled out. John Strachey's works are usually considered dynamite and it would probably be hard to find the works of Langston Hughes in southern libraries. As one prominent administrator said, "In this whole matter there is need for opportunism and compromise. The librarian as censor must try to represent the best and most enlightened public opinion. He should *perhaps* [italics in Otis] be a little in advance of his public," but not very much—and only *perhaps*. The "best and most enlightened opinion" which he strives to represent seldom reaches as far as the works of Marx, Lenin, Strachey, and Dutt.

—From *Forbidden Books in American Public Libraries, 1876–1939*,
by Evelyn Geller (Greenwood Press, 1984)

Busy Days During the Depression, public libraries took on a new significance as a refuge for the economically hard-pressed population. Not only were people after books that would help them deal with the crisis, but they needed books for entertainment and diversion. Bruce Weir Benidt in his history of the Minnesota Public Library, *The Library Book*, points out, "A 1934 study showed that between 1929 and 1933, the libraries of seventy-seven cities with populations of more than one hundred thousand jumped in circulation by twenty-three percent, 'while total expenditures dropped by an identical percentage.' "

Two photographs from the mid-1930s from Pittsburgh reflect those times: story hour at the Pennsylvania Avenue Branch *(top)* and an active reference reading room in the main library. A third *(overleaf top)* shows another example of the ever-popular story hour at the library, an institution which was thriving with, not suffering from, the story-telling abilities of radio. This was taken at the Henry E. Legler Regional library in Chicago. (Carnegie Library of Pittsburgh and Chicago Public Library)

Outdoor Reading Room Continuing interest in the fate of the impoverished and unemployed led the Minneapolis Public Library to set up an outdoor reading room in an area typified by cheap hotels and bars. It was in operation during the 1930s and 1940s. (Minneapolis Public Library)

A ROMANCE FOR CLASSIFIERS ONLY 1934

'Twas in the merry month of June, in a dewey seven-eleven,
A pretty girl beside the lake, idly watched the five-nine-seven.
The seven-five-two of autumn was a visual delight,
And she became one-hundred-ninety at the beauty of the sight.
But presently a nine-thirteen appeared, in style of recent date,
And as he passed, you'd think his neck was made of six-seven-eight.
The three-forty of attraction made him linger there at first:
"Wilt have a six-six-three," he asked, "to quench thy dainty thirst?"
"Or if perchance, six-forty-one is what your preference's for,
I'm sure that you and I could get some three-hundred-thirty-four."
Her scornful glance would surely wither anything alive.
"I may not have three-seventy, but I know my three-nine-five.
"I do not like your six-five-eight, your eight-fifteen is dirty,
"Your one-seventy is questionable, you tire my hundred-thirty.
"Your four-fifteen is terrible—" but the rest of it was lost;
For he fell upon the five-two-five, and there gave up the ghost.
The moral of this little tale is surely plain as fate—
If you frequent seven-elevens, you'll end in seven-one-eight.

A key to the above should not be necessary, but in case it is—

130—Mind and body
170—Ethics
190—Modern philosopher
334—Cooperation
340—Law
370—Education

395—Etiquette
415—Grammar
525—Earth
597—Fishes
641—Food
658—Business methods

663—Beverages
678—Rubber
711—Public parks
718—Cemeteries
815—Oratory
913—Antiquities

—From *The Wilson Bulletin for Librarians*, January 1934, by Elizabeth Collom

Modern Times For its part, the Library of Congress continued to pioneer new labor-saving devices during the Depression. This is the control room *(right)* for a pneumatic tube system used to carry books between the Main Library and its Annex, which opened in 1939. The new Annex was spartan in comparison to the original building, but it did have its finer points. One of them was this reading room *(opposite top)*, which is shown in a recent photograph. (Library of Congress)

The Making of a Cliché In the 1937 Republic movie *Navy Blues,* a sailor meets a prim, drab librarian who, in the course of the action, is charmed into taking off her glasses and letting her hair down to emerge as a ravishing beauty. The cliché may not have started here, but it was surely reinforced in this movie. (Museum of Modern Art Film Still Archives)

Attendant John Vachon captured this man at work in the newspaper reading room of the Omaha Public Library in 1938. (Library of Congress, FSA)

A EUROPEAN LIBRARIAN LOOKS AT THE BIG CITY LIBRARY 1939

When a European librarian comes to America on a study trip, he immediately directs his course toward the great and renowned million-dollar libraries and plans his itinerary with a view to taking in as many of them as possible. . . .

Nowhere else can one get a more vivid impression of what a composite mechanism a modern library really is. As seen by the public it is a book exhibit and a bookstore with hundreds of thousands of individually selected books on open shelves, a giant reading club with dozens of study rooms for specialists, an unrivaled newsstand, a book storehouse of international scope, a museum of rare books, an art gallery for prints and drawings, a civic forum and a folk high school with lecture hall and study circles, a Mecca for the blind, a monster kindergarten with picture books, story hours and a gold-fish pond. And from the inside it is an independent civil service institution, with hundreds of officials, assistants, secretaries and clerks, an information bureau, a bibliographical institute, a publicity agency, a supply depot for dozens of branches, sub-branches and school deposits, and a series of shops for binding, printing, carpentering and repairing.

The Crowning Glory of American Librarianship. That this whole system can function smoothly and without grating is due to the thorough and intricate organization of the work, from the janitor's routine and the lending mechanism right up to cataloging rules for the most subtle problems in the remotest languages. The large American city library is the crowning glory of American librarianship. . . . The public library of Boston, "the first free city library in the world supported by taxation," sticks to its old cultural traditions, even to the extent of still training its own personnel. The Chicago Public Library, on the other hand, has always remained a popular library (in the better sense of the word), leaving the humanities to the Newberry Library and the sciences to the John Crerar. Its white marble steps have been worn hollow by the millions who have come to seek recreation, relaxation and inspiration in books in all the languages of the world. Cleveland impresses one by its earnest work of serving the professionally interested through its fifteen departmental reading rooms. Philadelphia's library palace, in the style of Louis XV, gives an effect of artistry and dignified reserve. Its invitation is not to the man in the street. Detroit has erected "a cultural temple of all faiths" in a roaring industrial city. Baltimore's new library, built on the department store plan, is a natural expression of an enterprising publicity policy. Seattle's old-fashioned Carnegie building is swollen to bursting by the library's work of fulfilling its civic responsibility toward immigrants from two continents. Los Angeles with its pleasing and artistic reading rooms has hit upon the happy idea of focusing them about a rotunda where the activity rivals that of a southern European market place. I could go on, but let me close the list with the New York Public Library, whose main building on Fifth Avenue is the center of the world's largest library system, and in itself a departmentalized British Museum. Around each of these main libraries, like planets about the sun, there are branches scattered throughout the city—all functioning in accordance with the same laws, but each reflecting the specific social and racial features of the neighborhood.

—From *American Librarianship from a European Angle,* by William Munthe (American Library Association, 1939)

Backwoods Library Dorothea Lange
took this picture in the Piney Woods of
southwestern Mississippi in July of 1937
while documenting American life for the
Farm Security Administration. Like other
FSA photographs appearing on the next
few pages, Lange's photograph shows
the vitality and spirit of library life, first,
in the face of the Depression and, then,
at the onset of World War II. (Library of
Congress, FSA)

THE FORTIES
BOOKS
GO TO WAR

W hen the United States entered World War II, it was quickly decided as a matter of policy that the members of the armed forces, no matter where they were located, would not lack for morale-boosting reading material. In a matter of months, the United States Army put together, to quote an American Library Association publication of the 1940s, "the greatest free circulating library system which has ever existed." Many participated in the book mobilization; for instance, two ALA book drives netted 17 million books.

The growth of military libraries was offset to some degree by the fall-off in public library patronage. People claimed that they did not have as much time for reading, and many regular users were now in uniform. In fact, the percentage of the population registered in large public libraries was less in 1946 than in 1921. Not only was there a shortage of patrons, there were also staff shortages as members went to war. The Army alone had more than a thousand trained librarians in its system. Added to this were shortages of bookmobiles, gas, and tires as well as a lack of money for "general interest"

FIVE

books, as funds were diverted to what was most practical (war information, technical works, victory-garden manuals and other "how to" books).

After the War, things at home started to hum again. The GIs were home and needed books to fuel their postwar educations. A Midwestern librarian had to limit the time textbooks could be checked out after "students descended like grasshoppers on a Dakota wheat field, stripping the shelves bare before the astonished staff could gather themselves together. . . ." Others also began to see the library as an oasis of opportunity for, among other things, making money. This was driven home in the late 1940s when John Deferrari, the son of an immigrant fruit vendor, gave the Boston Public Library more than $1.5 million. At the time he remarked that he had become a multimillionaire by using the Statistical Room. A reporter for the *Boston Globe* asked him if anybody could do this. His answer: "Study the corporation reports like I did. Find out who's behind a business. Learn all about it, and then invest your money in the right ones."

Beginning in the 1935 and extending into 1942 some of the best photographers in America were assembled by Roy Stryker, who assigned them the task of documenting American life through programs established by the Farm Security Administration. It has been said that it was the greatest photographic team ever assembled and the 270,000 photographs that it produced are now combined with strong images from the Office of War Information in the FSA–OWI collection at the Library of Congress. The photographs on the next five pages were selected from that collection to show library life in the early 1940s.

New Mexico Sign *(opposite top)* on the side of a building in Mogollon, New Mexico, by Russell Lee. June 1940

California Girls *(opposite below)* reading a copy of *Popular Mechanics* at the library in the Farm Security Administration's farm workers' camp in Tulare County, California, by Russell Lee, February 1942.

Florida Students *(top left)* in the Bethune–Cookman College Library in Daytona Beach, Florida, by Gordon Parks, January 1943.

Washington, D.C. Woman *(top right)* in the reading room of a public library, by Esther Bubley, July 1943.

Arizona Farm Security Administration Library *(right)* in Yuma, by Russell Lee. March 1942.

Wisconsin Boy reading the funny papers *(right)* on the steps of the Public Library, Milwaukee, by John Vachon, July 1940.

Georgia Students *(below)* in the Atlanta University Library, by Arthur Rothstein, March 1942.

North Carolina Sgt. Williams *(opposite top)* in the library of the Service Club at Fort Bragg, by Arthur Rothstein, March 1942.

New York High school students *(opposite below)* visiting the library at a Batavia FSA farm labor camp by John Collier, September 1942.

Arizona In the small lending library of the Casa Grande Valley Farms, Pinal County, by Russell Lee, April 1940.

Virginia Officers of the School of Military Government in the Library of International Law at the University of Virginia, by John Collier, April 1943.

FROM THE DIARY OF A VILLAGE LIBRARY, FRANCESTOWN, NEW HAMPSHIRE 1943

June 19

My first day as librarian, and how I did enjoy it! Meeting the few persons who came in, finding out what they were interested in, and handing out books of their choice was my kind of fun. Books and people need more introducing than they sometimes get; here was a chance to see how much I could accomplish.

With war taking away many people to fight and carry on other kinds of work and giving us all many extra chores, and gas rationing keeping everyone off the road as much as possible, I can't expect reading to be up to normal—or maybe it will be increasing while people travel less. Last year's town appropriation for all Library expenses was $260. Only twenty books were bought, but the total circulation of books and magazines was 6,782; so we must be depending a great deal on gifts and the re-reading of old books. There are some good new ones, I see.

Since I am the whole staff, with no experience and no more knowledge of library techniques than I had learned by using city libraries in my early years, plus an hour a week one year in high school when the school librarian gave me instruction in library matters useful to a bookworm like me, I'll need to keep my mind on what I'm doing. Stamping books, checking the card numbers of patrons, and putting book cards back into returned books are chores repeated often enough so that they should become automatic in a reasonable time. There are pieces of paper on which to record fine money, which is used for such desk supplies as catalog cards, book pockets, and pencils. If there is any cash left from these expenses, I may buy a few books, for which I'll keep a list of wanted titles.

The sweeping of these three big rooms is to be part of my work (one of them is the equal of two), and the furnace in the basement is to be replenished with chunks of wood now and then. So here I am, mistress of all I survey: dirt, clutter, two closets full of moldy miscellaneous items, and shelves of shabby books. I'll try to earn my forty cents an hour.

October 6

There is a shortage of wood just now for the library furnace, but I keep myself comfortable with the fireplace. This doesn't encourage browsing by the patrons in the other rooms, though.

Surgical dressings are being made evenings upstairs in the room overhead by a group of Red Cross volunteers, and the register above me lets down their chatter and laughter while I try to find suitable numbers for books when not otherwise occupied. Messing around with white ink, trying to decide what a book is about, and waiting on patrons at the same time is more or less confusing. I may have to be satisfied with merely grouping books by subject on the shelves.

—From *Diary of a Village Library*, by Caroline M. Lord (New Hampshire Publishing Company, 1971)

General Stores Deposit libraries located in general stores continued to be popular in the 1940s. These two *(right top and bottom)* were located in stores in Michigan and Indiana. (Office of Education and ALA Archives)

Toy Library An early example of an idea that was to spread in the postwar years, this photograph *(opposite top left)* was taken in New York City in 1943 at school run by the Ethical Culture Society. (Free Library of Philadelphia)

Home Front In May 1942 this War Reading Room *(opposite bottom)* opened at the Washington, D.C., Public Library. It brought to one place all the material in the library needed by patrons interested in World War II and matters related to it. A similar effort *(opposite top right)* at the Carnegie Library of Pittsburgh is displayed under the slogan: ''Your public library in the war promotes family living.''

Such war-information rooms were common and in some cases supported by the WPA, which was still active at the beginning of the War. In Minnesota, for instance, there were more than 300 of these in operation by the end of 1942. At about the same time the WPA's State Chief for War Services in Minnesota spoke to the Minnesota Library Association and called for more. He wanted every library in the state to ''transform its facilities into an active war information center.'' The WPA man was Hubert H. Humphrey. (Martin Luther King Library and the Carnegie Library of Pittsburgh)

Victory Book Campaigns During 1942 and 1943 two massive drives were organized to collect books for members of the armed forces. These campaigns were started by the ALA, which sponsored them with the help of the American Red Cross and the United Service Organizations. Shown *(opposite top left)* are an early drive at the Chicago Public Library (1941), a Red Cross worker *(opposite top right)* collecting books, a book-drive rally in front of the New York Public Library *(opposite below)*, and *(above)* singer Kate Smith giving a copy of the official poster to Dr. Harry Wann, who chaired the drive. The poster designer looks on. Smith was the Honorary Chairman of the Radio Board of the campaign. (ALA Library)

Wartime Librarian Poet Archibald MacLeish served as Librarian of Congress from 1939 to 1944. His appointment was vigorously opposed by librarians, who felt the post should have been held by a professional. Some 1,400 librarians attending the ALA Convention in San Francisco in 1939 signed a petition opposing his appointment. (Library of Congress)

THE LIBRARIAN AND THE DEMOCRATIC PROCESS 1940

—

It would be a brave man and an optimistic man who would suggest at this hour that the events of the past few weeks and months have been anything but evil. Certainly it would be a very foolish librarian who would suggest that there was any countervailing circumstance to balance the armed successes of obscurantism and brutal force. But there is, I think, one consequence of all this evil which may perhaps be turned to good, and not least by those who keep the libraries of this country. No one can look at Spain, at Austria, at Czechoslovakia, at Poland, at Finland, at Denmark, at Norway, at Holland, at Belgium and at the situation in Europe of France and Great Britain without asking himself with a new intensity, a new determination to be answered, how our own democracy can be preserved.

And no one can ask with earnestness and intelligence how our own democracy can be preserved without asking at the very outset how his own work, his own activity, can be shaped to that end. Librarians will ask that question of themselves as others will. And asking it, they may perhaps arrive at certain conclusions as to themselves and their relations to the life of the country which will be valuable not only to the country but to themselves as well. Specifically they may perhaps arrive at certain conclusions as to the great question which, in speech and in silence, explicitly and implicitly, has troubled them so long—the question of their profession.

The wholly admirable attempt to put librarianship upon a professional basis, has, as I understand it, met this principal difficulty: that it has proved impossible to arrive at a common agreement as to the social end which librarianship exists to serve. Men are bound together in professions not because they speak in professional vocabularies or share professional secrets or graduate from professional schools. Men are bound together in professions because they devote themselves in common to the performance of a function of such social importance—a function so difficult, so particular, and so essential to the welfare of society—that it requires of necessity a discipline, a technique, and even an ethic of its own. The definition of that function in the case of librarianship has not proved easy. The social function of the medical profession is known to every member of that profession. The social function of the profession of the law was well known to lawyers in the years before the law became a business. But the ablest and most distinguished librarians declare without hesitation that they have not themselves arrived at a statement of the function of librarianship satisfactory to themselves, nor have their colleagues supplied the lack. . . .

There are dangers in such an undertaking. But there are dangers also—even greater dangers—in refusing to attempt it. And the rewards of success are rewards worth seeking. Not only would the cause of democracy, the cause we believe to be the cause of civilization, be served. But it is conceivable that the profession to which we belong might find in the process the definition of its function for which it has sought so long—a function as noble as any men have ever served.

—From *Champion of a Cause*, by Archibald MacLeish (American Library Association, 1971)

The most spectacular library development during the War was the explosive expansion of library services to members of the armed forces. The Army made the headlines, but others participated in the boom. The Navy boosted its corps of librarians in uniform from a mere 15 before the War to 450. Expenditures for service libraries jumped from less than $500,000 in 1940 to $3.9 million in 1945.

Books for GIs A major effort was made to get books to American servicemen during World War II. Visual evidence of this includes:

(Right top) Soldiers being given books at Camp Robinson, Arkansas, in a picture released by the Signal Corps in 1942 to show that such libraries were "badly in need" of more books. (Defense Audiovisual Agency)

(Right below) Troops in a library set up by the Red Cross on the island of Bougainville in the South Pacific in 1944. (DAA)

(Overleaf top) The cozy, well-lit military library in Adak, Alaska, in 1944. (DAA)

(Overleaf bottom) In a crude Special Services library in Ledo, Assam, India. (DAA)

(Overleaf opposite top) Books being crated in Hawaii for shipment to the troops in Guam in 1945. An Army librarian temporarily occupies one of the boxes. (DAA)

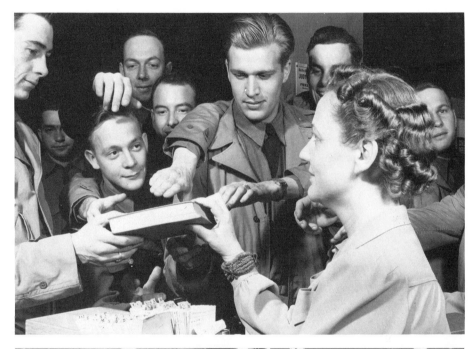

Victory Parade General Dwight D.
Eisenhower and Mayor Fiorello
LaGuardia pass *(opposite below)* in front of
the New York Public Library at the end
of the War. As previous photographs
have shown, the library became a major
rallying point for book drives in both
World Wars. (New York Public Library)

Jeepmobile Two views of a special Jeep–
bookmobile created for the military. Each
special trailer held 500 books. These
pictures were taken in Rheims, France,
in late 1945. (DAA)

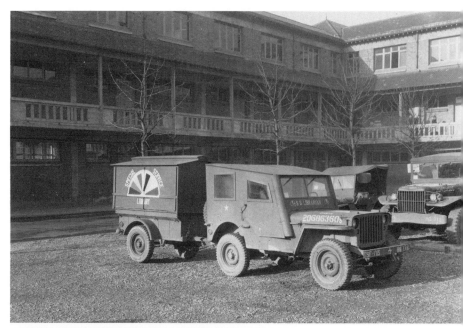

ON THE FRONT WITH WODEHOUSE AND WAUGH WORLD WAR II

Then, in connection with World War II, the post library at Camp Livingston, Louisiana, was my next hangout. I was editing a mimeographed regimental newspaper, and used the library (it was well stocked, and all the books were pristine) to research a series of articles about great humorists, a series that I'm sure baffled my fellow-soldiers, but pleased me immensely. I also sat in for the librarian from time to time, and learned Mr. Dewey's system. Shortly thereafter, at a sultry camp on the Florida coast, and at another sweltering one near Richmond, Virginia, I built up a regimental library of a couple of thousand scruffy books rounded up from helpful citizens, and established myself in a large, dank tent which doubled as the publishing office for my paper. It was also the goof-off place for myself and my friends to take naps, so it served a triple morale purpose. When we moved overseas from Richmond, I found an immense wooden crate, easily the size of four coffins, and convinced the officer in charge that the library had to move with us. I well remember the terrible time eight husky soldiers had moving that box, and a dozen others hoisting it onto a truck, and the murderous looks they gave me—the librarian.

Once in Europe, the giant box and its companions mysteriously disappeared for eight months while we were stationed in a Welsh castle, but just as mysteriously reappeared when we moved to an encampment on Salisbury Plain. There I once again persuaded those in charge to let me run a library, and I set up the books in a ramshackle tin building placed oddly in the middle of a sort of parade ground; I further managed to get permission to sleep in the building to avoid theft. (The only book ever stolen was Waugh's *Vile Bodies*—and surely for the wrong reasons.) My fellow soldiers slept in cramped tents on the periphery of the parade ground, and every morning they were aroused at six to do calisthenics and police the area—pick up cigarette butts and other small debris. I got the feeling that they resented my library when they started kicking the reverberating sides of my building on their policing missions, snarling things like "Lazy bum!" and "Wake up, Cole!"

LIBRARY STUDIES WITH GERTRUDE STEIN

There were about fifty worthwhile books in the library: some Graham Greene, Wodehouse, Waugh, Mencken, Hemingway, and a few poetry anthologies; and these I kept in circulation, pressing them on the sometimes unwilling customers. Truly a "personal" librarian. We moved to France a week after D-Day, leaving my library to who knows what fate. Then, immediately after the war ended, I was stationed in Germany, and the question came up, "Would you like to go to library school in Paris for two weeks?" Hah! Would I? And I, a mere corporal, was given a jeep and driver and sent off. There was no library to train me for, mind you, nor none in prospect, but somebody higher up had decided that the Army just might need some semi-librarians some time in the future, so I found myself one of fifty happy soldiers attending classes at Cité Universitaire, learning how to alphabetize, which is about all that was taught. But we did have a fascinating afternoon with Gertrude Stein and—need it be said— Alice B. Toklas. I remember looking out the window and seeing Gertrude and Alice sitting majestically in the back seat of a jeep drawing into the courtyard. I can't remember a thing Stein said, but she was a riveting presence. Alice Toklas sat knitting throughout in the last seat in the classroom.

—From *American Libraries*, April 1976, by William Cole

After the Hostilities The determination to get books to Americans in the armed forces continued in the late 1940s. These libraries are in such far-flung locations as the *USS Olympus* in the Antarctic *(right)*; on the island of Guam *(below)*; and in a quonset hut *(opposite top)* on Okinawa. (DAA)

Hospital Service Using a native *kargahan*, Sophie Fair *(opposite below)* of the Army Special Services totes books to the wards of a military hospital in the Philippines in 1947. In the period just after the War, a major effort was made to make sure that military and Veterans Administration hospitals had access to libraries. In 1947, the VA could point to the fact that it employed hundreds of librarians overseeing a network of 124 patient libraries and another 138 medical and administrative staff libraries (DAA)

The Silver Screen Among others, these motion pictures of the era featured libraries and librarians. In *Quiet Please, Murder* (1942) much of the mystery is set in a library. The story involves a plot by a master forger, played by a dapper George Sanders *(right)*, who plans to steal a rare volume of Shakespeare and then make copies, which he will pass off to greedy collectors as the original. In Frank Capra's *It's a Wonderful Life* (1946) the late Donna Reed *(below)* was cast as a librarian. (Museum of Modern Art Film Still Archives)

Recruiting After hearing a critic call the librarians "overly feminine, segregated and timid," young-adult librarian Margaret A. Edwards of the Enoch Pratt decided to recruit young readers in areas where juvenile delinquency was high and the circulation of books low. In an effort to attract those readers, Edwards put her Book Wagon on the road in the mid-1940s. Two photographs *(opposite)* from 1945 show the wagon in the streets and a third *(opposite bottom right)* shows one of the horses used to pull the wagon with a temporary handler. The horse was called Berry (as in "Liberry"). In one thirty-eight-day period, 725 new members were registered and over 4,000 books were circulated. (Enoch Pratt Free Library)

146

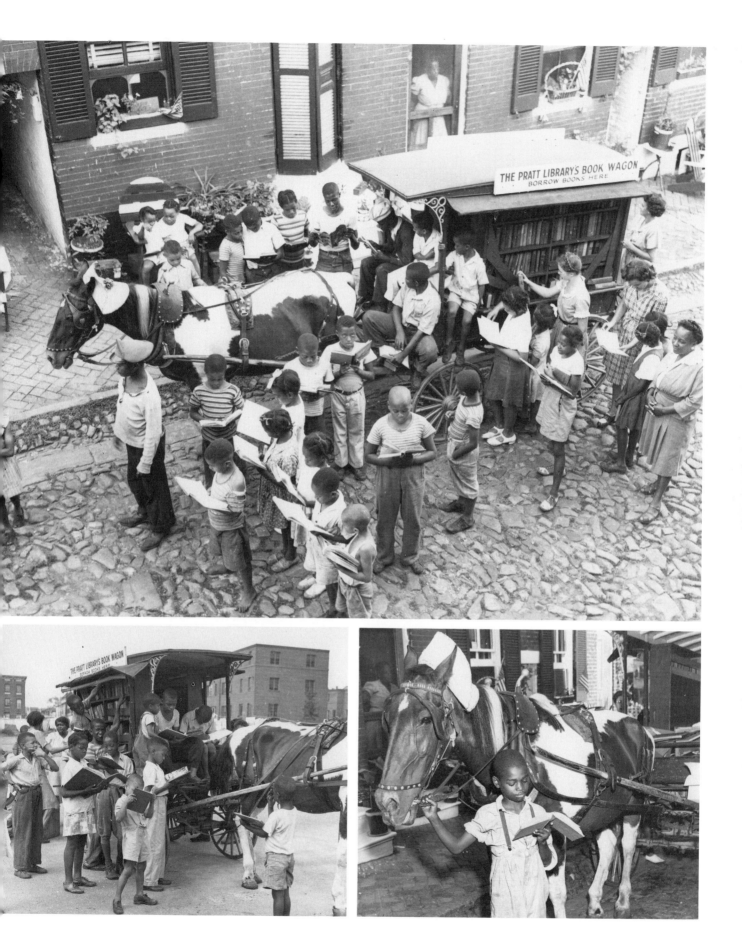

THE PRATT LIBRARY'S BOOK WAGON
BORROW BOOKS HERE

147

Horseless The Enoch Pratt was also beginning to put motorized vehicles on the road in the late 1940s. Others were just starting bookmobile programs as well. In fact, the first one in Southern California did not take to the road until February 7, 1949, when the Los Angeles Public Library sent one out. (Enoch Pratt Free Library)

Distinguished Visitor Helen Keller during her visit to the Library of Congress Division for the Blind in 1947. Then, as now, the Library of Congress had a profound impact on the visually handicapped. Currently the Library produces some two million Braille and recorded books a year. (Library of Congress)

Under the Palms Free Library operated by the Los Angeles Public Library in Pershing Square Park, 1949. (National Archives)

Anthracite Anthems Miners in Centralia, Pennsylvania, being recorded by the Library of Congress's Archive of American Folk Song. Although the recorded collection dated back to 1928, when four individuals gave a thousand dollars apiece to start, it was not until the 1940s, when this picture was taken, that records were pressed and sold to the public. (Library of Congress)

In the Snow In 1949 the United States Information Agency collected photographs to show elements of American life, including the traditions of the public library, to people visiting information centers in other parts of the world. Two collected from Vermont *(above left and right)* are these images of a "Bookwagon" operated by the Montpelier Region Free Public Library Commission and the 160-year-old Martha Canfield Library in Arlington, Vermont, which was founded for the simple purpose of buying "a larger supply of books than one could individually afford to own." (National Archives)

Chicago Story Pictures collected by the U.S. government in 1949 to show the workings of a modern urban library system came from Chicago and include the main reading room *(opposite top)*, where more than a half-million questions were answered annually; games being run for children *(right)* during the summer months; and one of 172 deposit points for books around the city—this one *(opposite bottom)* in a hospital. (National Archives)

Visitors Ten young men and women from England arrive in the United States in the summer of 1949 to participate in the International Farm Youth Exchange Project and make a stop at the Boston Public Library in Copley Square. (National Archives)

Atomic Age A 1948 display at the Enoch Pratt Free Library in Baltimore underscoring a new concern of postwar library patrons. Echoing the optimism of the era, the original caption on this photo promises, "With full understanding of atomic energy, the world will choose prosperity and peacetime progress." (National Archives)

LIBRARIANS
versus
AUTHORS
1945

Considering the fact that authors are, so to speak, an essential raw material of the library profession, it is hard to imagine that librarians would deliberately go out of their way to irritate them. Illogical and unbelievable as it may seem, however, librarians have declared an all-out war against those who make their profession possible. The evidence of this titanic but silent struggle is right there on the library catalog card; it shows not only that the fight goes on but that thus far librarians have had the upper hand.

First, there is the anti-social practice of librarians using dates of birth and death for authors. It is generally agreed that in polite society a person's age is his own business; but does the librarian recognize the author's right to his little secret? Oh, no! The librarian noses here and there and digs and searches until finally she discovers the birth date and plasters it right on the top of the catalog card!

OVER TWENTY-ONE

How many lady librarians who bandy people's birth dates about without giving the matter a thought would want their age on file in one of the most public of all public places—the public library? . . . One can't help wondering how many books have remained unwritten or at least unpublished because the authors or potential authors hesitated to have one of their most cherished secrets bared by busy-body librarians who just couldn't rest until somehow they managed to discover when the author first saw the light of day. . . . Just picture a librarian spending her time and your money unsuccessfully trying to discover when Susie Smith, who has just published a children's book called *Lemmie, the Lemur*, was born—a fact of life which is the purely private and personal business of Miss Susie Smith. (How many children do you know who ever asked anybody when the author of their picture book was born?) This librarian has searched in all the places where librarians search for such choice morsels of knowledge and she has been frustrated at every turn. Here is an author who has kept her secret well! So what happens to Miss Smith? Her name appears at the head of the catalogue card without any date. Now that would be fine if every other name in the catalog had no dates but since authors filed before and after "Smith, Susie" do have dates, what does the catalog tell us about the kind Miss Smith (who never would have got into this mess if she hadn't written a book to make children happy and give librarians something to do)? It tells us that she is so gosh-darned old that she is afraid to divulge her age!

This question of dates brings up yet another way that librarians have devised to torment authors; I refer to the jolly trick of placing a dash after the birth date of living authors (Smith, John, 1900–   ). Of all the grisly, ghastly, gruesome practices! There are the author's name, his date of birth, and that dash! That dash creates a funereal and mortuary atmosphere which has no place anywhere except in an undertaking establishment. An author seeing himself on a library card with the dash ready and waiting for what follows must have chills run up and down his spine. It's like seeing one's own tombstone with all the information on it except that last final date.

—From *Publisher's Weekly*, January 13, 1945, by Samuel Sass

THE FIFTIES
ROLLING
FORWARD

Fears about television were unfounded, and library circulation reached all-time highs in cities and counties around the country. In fact, it seemed that television had a positive effect on libraries. In 1956 when the District of Columbia compiled its report for 1955, it not only noted that for the first time book circulation had gone over two million but added that television was serving to introduce many people to reading. Nineteen fifty-five was the "Year of Davy Crockett," and the influence of the TV series had driven all sorts

SIX

of people to the library. One D.C. librarian was quoted in the *Washington Star* on the phenomenon: "Nothing has ever rung in our ears with such vehemence as the cries for Davy Crockett—from all ages and both sexes." Other concerns luring people into their libraries ranged from a fascination with "high fidelity" to concern over the effect of comic books on young people.

On the negative side, there was a growing trend toward the banning of books in communities across the country. It had begun in the late 1940s with such actions as several boards of education banning *The Nation* magazine and the Philadelphia vice squad raiding bookstores to seize pornographic books, including works by William Faulkner. By the early 1950s, some efforts reached an absurd level, such as a bill introduced in the Texas legislature that would have barred funds for any state-supported institution with books in its library that "poke fun at the United States or the Lone Star State or which ridicule any American or Texas heroes." Books actually did get burned, and the climate was such that books and pamphlets that were anti-Communist were banned for not hitting hard enough. "The thinking of some Americans who would fight communism by creating a noisome censorship apparatus is difficult of analysis," wrote Donald Michael Rauh in a 1953 article on the situation. "But it is quite clear that the ranks of the literary vigilantes are rapidly swelling."

The Library Bill of Rights, first adopted by the ALA Council in 1939 and amended in 1948, was clearly against this kind of censorship and became a weapon in the fight to stem it.

On Wheels In the 1950s, libraries found new means of delivering, handling, and getting back books. In Cincinnati, a library employee receives a book at a thoroughly modern drive-in window *(right)*. A young Iowan *(below)* uses a drive-up book bin, courtesy of the Cedar Rapids Public Library. In Louisville, the Free Public Library takes a hint *(opposite top left and right)* from the supermarket by putting shopping carts in the aisles. (Office of Education and National Archives)

New Demands A critic once discharged the public library as "a mundane place where books are kept." If it was ever true, it was becoming less so in the 1950s, as libraries took on new functions and services. Patrons wanted more than a few books to take home and demanded more: books on emerging technology, a place to work, a center for seminars and lectures, and a source of advice in dealing with specifics ranging from the proper rearing of children to the successful completion of weekend do-it-yourself projects. In photographs of the time *(opposite, bottom left and right)* a visitor to the Carnegie Library of Pittsburgh checks out new technical books and users of the Cleveland Public Library make use of typewriters in a room next to the Technology Division. (Carnegie Library of Pittsburgh and *Library Journal*, photo by Frances Kacala)

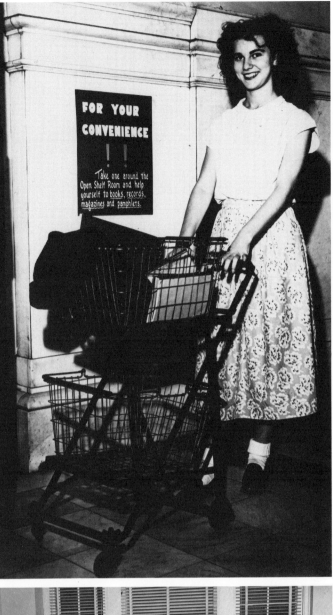

157

Spies and Reds Two films which reflected the Cold War climate and involved libraries appeared in the 1950s. In a 1951 Signal Corps movie, *Face to Face with Communism*, Communist leaders *(top right)* address the people from the steps of the library in an American country town. In the 1952 film *The Thief* the card catalog at the Library of Congress is used by couriers and agents passing messages and microfilm. In this scene *(bottom right)*, an innocent bystander—the woman in the middle—almost interrupts the passing of a message between Ray Milland and Martin Gabel. This spy movie was something of a novelty because it contained no dialogue. Critics said the gimmick wore thin after a few minutes. (U.S. Army and MOMA Film Still Archives)

Korean Service once again, the military worked hard to provide books and librarians for a war zone. By 1952 the Army controlled a chain of nearly 600 libraries worldwide—three quarters of which were housed in Army buildings. These were not makeshift affairs but professional libraries run by professionals.

Librarians from all over Korea pose *(opposite top)* for a group photo on December 9, 1953. The meeting was held to discuss "proper procedures in library work." Checkout procedures seem to be working properly as GIs borrow books *(opposite below left)* from a 25th Infantry Division bookmobile. Back in San Francisco, special Armed Forces paperback editions of popular books were packed *(opposite, below right)* for soldiers at the front. These books, being packed—315 titles to a kit—in late November of 1950, were to be delivered to fighting units at the front before New Year's. These cheap but legible 3″ × 6″ paperbacks were first issued in World War II by the Council on Books in Wartime, which produced them for a mere six cents a copy. Many millions were distributed. (DAA)

Railroad Library In Korea this aging railroad car *(below)* was turned into a center for information and education. These pictures of the rather unusual library were taken in April 1954. This train-car library was not, however, unprecedented, since in the days before bookmobiles, several railroads had created rolling libraries for their workers. (DAA)

THE FREEDOM TO READ 1953

1. It is in the public interest for publishers and librarians to make available the widest diversity of views and expressions, including those which are unorthodox or unpopular with the majority.
2. Publishers, librarians, and booksellers do not need to endorse every idea or presentation contained in the books they make available. It would conflict with the public interest for them to establish their own political, moral, or aesthetic views as a standard for determining what books should be published or circulated.
3. It is contrary to the public interest for publishers or librarians to determine the acceptability of a book on the basis of the personal history or political affiliations of the author.
4. There is no place in our society for efforts to coerce the taste of others, to confine adults to the reading matter deemed suitable for adolescents, or to inhibit the efforts of writers to achieve artistic expression.
5. It is not in the public interest to force a reader to accept with any book the prejudgment of a label characterizing the book or author as subversive or dangerous.
6. It is the responsibility of publishers and librarians, as guardians of the people's freedom to read, to contest encroachments upon that freedom by individuals or groups seeking to impose their own standards or tastes upon the community at large.
7. It is the responsibility of publishers and librarians to give full meaning to the freedom to read by providing books that enrich the quality and diversity of thought and expression. By the exercise of this affirmative responsibility, bookmen can demonstrate that the answer to a bad book is a good one, the answer to a bad idea is a good one.

The freedom to read is of little consequence when expended on the trivial; it is frustrated when the reader cannot obtain matter fit for his purpose. What is needed is not only the absence of restraint, but the positive provision of opportunity for the people to read the best that has been thought and said. Books are the major channel by which the intellectual inheritance is handed down, and the principal means of its testing and growth. The defense of their freedom and integrity, and the enlargement of their service to society, requires of all bookmen the utmost of their faculties, and deserves of all citizens the fullest of their support.

We state these propositions neither lightly nor as easy generalizations. We here stake out a lofty claim for the value of books. We do so because we believe that they are good, possessed of enormous variety and usefulness, worthy of cherishing and keeping free. We realize that the application of these propositions may mean the dissemination of ideas and manners of expression that are repugnant to many persons. We do not state these propositions in the comfortable belief that what people read is unimportant. We believe rather that what people read is deeply important; that ideas can be dangerous; but that the suppression of ideas is fatal to a democratic society. Freedom itself is a dangerous way of life, but it is ours.

—Full text of a statement originally issued by the Westchester Conference of the ALA and the Book Publisher's Council. Adopted June 25, 1953, and revised in 1972 by the ALA Council.

Islands It was hard to find a part of the United States without bookmobiles by the 1950s. Here is a school-library bookmobile in Hawaii *(right)* and another in Puerto Rico *(below)*—before and after *(opposite)* young patrons visit. In 1955 there were about a thousand bookmobiles in the United States, but that number began to climb steadily after the passage of the Library Services Act. Enacted in 1956, its prime purpose was to aid in bringing library service to rural areas and the bookmobile was seen as the ideal vehicle for this task. (Office of Education and Philadelphia Free Library)

Dolls Three young patrons arrive at the Logan Branch of the Free Library of Philadelphia for a special story hour devoted to literary dolls. As was the custom in many towns, these events were held early in the year so that new Christmas dolls could attend. (Free Library of Philadelphia)

Paragons This *(opposite top left)* was the Model Children's Library assembled for an exhibit at the Pennsylvania Academy of Fine Arts in 1955; also, the Children's Room at the Enoch Pratt *(opposite top left)* as it looked in 1952. (Free Library of Philadelphia—Bond–McGarry Studios and Enoch Pratt Free Library)

Publicity! Shown here putting the finishing touches on a 1954 Book Week billboard outside Philadelphia's City Hall *(opposite below)* is the director of the Free Library, Emerson Greenaway. Santa gives books for the newest bookmobile *(right)* in the Philadelphia fleet to Deborah Dillworth, daughter of the mayor-elect in 1955. (Free Library of Philadelphia)

REPORT FROM A PRISON LIBRARY 1955

A prison library is a route of escape from the routine of an imprisoned man's daily life.

In books the man inside the walls may travel—as a reader to far places with strange names. He can become, for the length of a story, a swash-buckling hero. For a while he can forget the high walls, iron bars, whistles, bells and depression of prison existence. At will, he becomes the cowboy, the knight-at-arms, the Indian-fighter, the clever lawyer, the self-sacrificing doctor. A nascent interest in a new skill, curiosity regarding something his cellmate said the night before, or perhaps a dream of finding a better way to a better life—all send him seeking knowledge, entertainment and help from the library shelves.

The most evident factor revealed by the records of any prison library is that, as far as reading habits and interests are concerned, the inside readers are not so very different from the folks outside.

But convicts are great readers of adventure. It seems as though their present circumscribed lives prod them incessantly toward new horizons, new worlds of conquest and exploration.

Walk into the library office. Ask the librarian for some firsthand information.

"How many books do we have in the library?"

He has a quick answer to this one. "At present, there are some 22,210 volumes on the shelves. Fiction totals 11,276; the other 10,934 are non-fiction." The librarian gives the figures rather proudly, as would a man who takes pride in his work and accomplishments.

"How many of our men make use of the library facilities?"

The librarian consults a file. About 25 percent use the library regularly, 25 percent use it with a fair degree of regularity, another 25 percent read occasionally, and the remainder do little, or no, reading."

To satisfy yourself, you ask: "Is it true that most convicts read nothing but fiction—adventure, western or detective stories?"

"Completely wrong. Only approximately 5 percent of library users here read nothing but fiction. In compiling progress reports, it has been noted that the men of average intelligence mix their reading. That is, they read about an equal number of fiction and nonfiction books. . . ."

. . . you ask another question: "What authors, or single author, is most in current demand in Atlanta?"

Another file consultation: "Well, first of all, Zane Grey and, secondly, Earl Stanley Gardner. We have over 40 titles by Gardner in 276 volumes and right now there are less than 60 of Gardner's books on the shelves."

"What is the most popular current title?"

"*From Here to Eternity*. We have 15 copies of it, have had a waiting list on it for over 2 years, and are just now catching up to the demand for it. I would say that over 600 men have read the Jones book here.

"Our other most popular book, oddly enough, is *Successful Marriage*, a compilation of writings of about 15 specialists, edited by Morris Fishbein. We have 7 copies and they have been on request for over 6 years. I would say, conservatively, that several hundred men have read it since we've had it in the library."

—From the Fall 1955 issue of *The Atlantian*, the magazine of the federal prison in Atlanta, by H. Lee White, inmate.

Books Behind Bars Two prison libraries at Federal installations. Shown are the libraries at the U.S. penitentiaries at Terre Haute, Indiana *(above)*, and Lewisburg, Pennsylvania. When Lewisburg opened in 1932, it not only had an inmate library, but it had been built into the original design specifications. Such fine-looking places were—and still are—a far cry from run-of-the-mill prison libraries.

On The Hill Among the many distinguished visitors to the Library of Congress during the 1950s were Mr. and Mrs. John O'Hara *(opposite top left)* and Robert Frost *(right)*, shown here in front of a portrait of himself that appeared in a 1955 exhibit devoted to his life. (Library of Congress)

Cincinnati's Best Built at a cost of $4.6 million and completed in 1955, the Public Library of Cincinnati and Hamilton County featured all that was modern including fluorescent and incandescent lighting. (Ray Leedy Collection)

Coolidge Not all of the fine special collections were going into the large central libraries. Immediately following his nomination for vice-president, the Forbes Library in Northampton, Massachusetts, began collecting material relating to this former resident. A special room was set aside for the collection in the mid-1950s. Shown here *(above right)* at the 1956 dedication: Mrs. Calvin Coolidge, John Coolidge, Cynthia Coolidge, Lydia Coolidge and Mrs. John Coolidge. It was the last public appearance of the former First Lady. (Forbes Library)

Dickens Leslie C. Staples of London, who is the editor of the *Dickensian*, signs a guest book in the Rare Book Room of the Free Library of Philadelphia, as he prepares to examine the Dickens Collection. (Free Library of Philadelphia)

Big Vans The ideal bookmobile of the 1950s was a big one with plenty of room inside for patrons to move around. This monster from Denver *(right)* was so big that it was called a Traveling Branch. As if to show its capacity, young students line up *(below)* to enter a Philadelphia bookmobile, while another giant *(opposite top)* serves four counties in North Dakota. A patron makes her selection in a bookmobile from Cedar Rapids, Iowa *(opposite bottom left)*, and a group enjoys "The Pied Piper Bookmobile" *(opposite bottom right)*, operated for children by the St. Louis Public Library. (Denver Public Library, Free Library of Philadelphia, and Office of Education)

Reading Machines In the Microfilm Room in the Carnegie Library of Pittsburgh, a patron *(above left)* is shown using the latest in library hardware while another *(top right)* reads the paper in the old-fashioned manner. (Carnegie Library of Pittsburgh) This patron *(right)* is absorbing the daily news at the Free Library of Philadelphia (Free Library of Philadelphia).

Extended Horizons Two images display the ever-broadening influence and interests of American libraries: the library at McMurdo Sound, Antarctica *(top right);* and the inside of a bookmobile *(above),* with a sign that reads "Our Library Now Has the Latest Books on SPUTNIKS. Scientific and Easy to Understand. The Future Belongs to Those Who Prepare for It." The Space Age had begun and one of the results was a burgeoning interest in technical subjects, which contributed to the library boom. (National Archives and Office of Education)

New Digs A model of the new Minneapolis Library is examined in 1958 by librarian Ray Williams (left) and his assistant. It opened two years later, replete with a major planetarium, which is seen here as the silvery dome in the foreground. (Minneapolis Public Library)

THE SIXTIES BORROWED TIME

"Negroes have won their fight to use the Greenville Public Library." So began an Associated Press article of September 19, 1960. "City and library officials announced it will open today on a integrated basis. It was closed two weeks ago after seven Negro students sued to end what they called discrimination solely on the basis of race at a facility supported by public tax money."

A movement that had begun in the late 1950s was continuing, as one segregated library after another was integrated. Many did it in a quiet manner. In 1959 Atlanta's system (the central library and its fourteen white and three black branches) were integrated without fuss after, to quote a wire service account, "a few Negroes visited the big downtown public library without attracting attention or causing any disturbance."

SEVEN

Meanwhile, the early 1960s also saw more new circulation records set all over the country, right up through the middle of the decade. Then circulation began to drop nationwide. All sorts of reasons were put forward—the effect of paperback books, the widespread improvement in school libraries, changing tastes, and population patterns, to name a few—but no clearcut reason emerged. Library professionals were perplexed. In 1966 one librarian told *Library Journal*, "With the largest book budget in history, and with an increasing population and a higher degree of literacy, it would seem that book use would be rapidly increasing instead of the slow but steady decrease." The result of the frustration was a widespread call for a renewed dedication to a librarianship that would include new efforts to reach the poor and disillusioned.

Sit-In: Jackson, Mississippi In April 1961 students began a series of "read-ins" at the public library. The first nine were hauled off to jail, the next group was tear-gassed as they marched downtown, and when the first nine came up for trial, blacks who had come to cheer them were gassed and set upon by police dogs. The first nine were fined $100 and given 30-day suspended sentences. The appeals for their case became the first legal attack on the state's segregation statutes. This scene shows the students being arrested. (*Library Journal* / Jackson *Daily News* photo)

Services for the Blind Philadelphia's old Library for the Blind was closed in 1972 and replaced with a new branch, but these photographs from the 1960s remind us of its vitality. Here is the staff *(opposite, top left)* posed on the steps of the old building; blind schoolchildren using the library *(opposite below)*; the magazine rack for blind patrons *(opposite, top right)*; and blind Girl Scouts during a 1966 visit *(above)*. Today the Library for the Blind and Physically Handicapped serves some 12,000 patrons throughout the Commonwealth of Pennsylvania through the mails. (Free Library of Philadelphia)

English Teacher If the patrons were new ones, their demands were not. They were the newly arrived, who saw the library as a place to learn English. The photograph is from 1964, but could have been taken in 1954 or 1984. The demand continues. (*Library Journal* by Ann Zane Shanks)

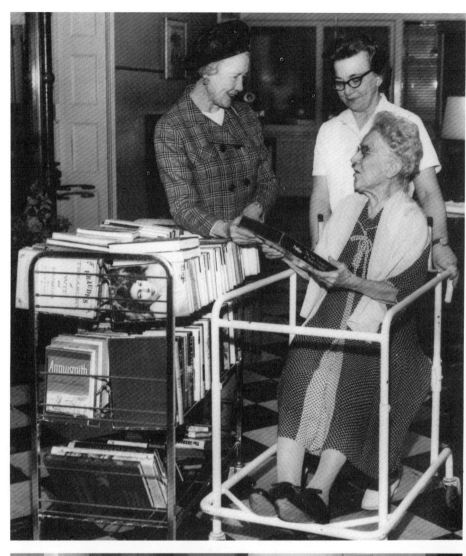

Service to the Aged As the bedside television set and paperback book racks at the lobby gift shop continued to sap the strength of library service to hospitals, attempts were made to reach the residents of nursing homes and other facilities housing old people. This picture from 1968 shows a member of the staff of the St. Louis Public Library helping a nursing-home patient select a book. (*Library Journal* / St. Louis Public Library)

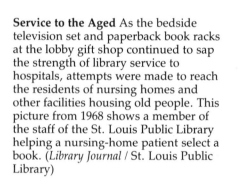

Recruiting As the library circulation boom continued through the early 1960s, there was a shortage of librarians, and efforts, such as this drive at the Free Library of Philadelphia in 1963, were made to recruit new ones. All of this was to change as circulation fell and tax dollars for libraries became harder to find. In 1979 Margaret K. Goggin, dean of the University of Denver's Graduate School of Librarianship, was quoted in the *New York Times*, "Back in the 1960's a librarian who was breathing could find a job, but then in the late 1960's and in the 1970's jobs became difficult to find." (Free Library of Philadelphia)

THE MOLESWORTH INSTITUTE 1963

As the result of numerous inquiries concerning the activities of the Molesworth Institute in recent months, the board of directors of the Institute with considerable reluctance has authorized publication of this brief article describing its basic goals and some of its library-oriented projects.

The Molesworth Institute was founded in 1956 as a privately supported nonprofit organization. Its basic objectives are to foster the growth and development of Molesworth studies in the United States, to combat the subversive and antihuman activities of the Treens, to encourage the spread of general knowledge and raise the general standard of intelligence throughout the world, and to destroy the basic fabric of bibliography. Our research workers, who are dedicated to these objectives, serve entirely on a volunteer basis, working on particular projects which they feel will best meet these objectives. For that reason, and because the Institute is interested only in pure research and will not accept financial aid from outside sources, work on most projects proceeds slowly and we do not envisage their completion in the near future. . . .

. . . Our major efforts to date have been devoted to publishing projects. First, we plan to solve a major space problem for libraries by microfilming all Braille books, perhaps the bulkiest of all library items. Second, we are preparing an octolingual interlinear edition of the famous 1721 Chinese encyclopedia, the *Ku Kin T'u Shu Thi' Ch'eng,* which was originally published in 5020 volumes. For some time, a team of outstanding world scholars have been translating this major work into English, French, Spanish, Russian, Arabic, Swahili, and Treen. The Chinese text will be reproduced from the original wood blocks. Our third project is the publication of all books from the long-lost *Librairie Saint Victor,* which were recently rediscovered in the basement of the Vladivostok Free Public Library. This will include, among other titles, *La Gualimaffree des Bigotz* and *L'Histoire des Farfaditz.*

Perhaps our major project, completed but lacking publication funds, is a periodical designed to amaze and confound the bibliographic world. This periodical, to be issued at the whim of the editor, will be entitled, purely and simply, *Ibid.* Its format will be so plain that it will be impossible to distinguish reference to it from other, more legitimate references using the term *Ibid.* In other words, by properly citing the periodical *Ibid.,* with or without page references, any statement appearing in it can be attributed to any author. All of our articles, untitled and unsigned, naturally, will be brief, general, and of the highest literary quality. In an effort to further confusion and spread the influence of *Ibid.,* each subscriber may make whatever corrections or additions he desires to the contents of any issue. . . .

The Institute's nonlibrary-oriented projects are equally important, but cannot be mentioned here. Suggestions for other projects of value to libraries that would further the aims of the Institute are always welcome, as are research workers who are willing to devote their time and energy to any of our ongoing projects.

—From the *ALA Bulletin* (1963), by Norman D. Stevens

VIPs Among the many notable visitors to the Library of Congress during the decade were Gregory Peck *(above)* and poet Robert Lowell *(above right).* The actor was there to study the motion-picture collection at the Library, while the poet was there to give a reading. (Library of Congress)

Good Skate In the 1966 Francis Ford Coppola film *You're a Big Boy Now,* the hero, who works in the stacks at the New York Public Library, uses roller skates to get around. Art was imitating life, because a 1965 *Time* article on how libraries were trying to keep up with the explosion of information reported that the Detroit Public Library was giving its workers skates so they could move more quickly down the 250-foot-long stacks. (Museum of Modern Art Film Still Archives)

Marion Shirley Jones as River City's Marion the Librarian in *The Music Man* (1962). If the character and her library reinforced some of the shopworn library clichés (note the shushing in this scene), Jones was an agreeable character and a far cry from some of the sterner librarians of fiction. (MOMA Film Still Archives)

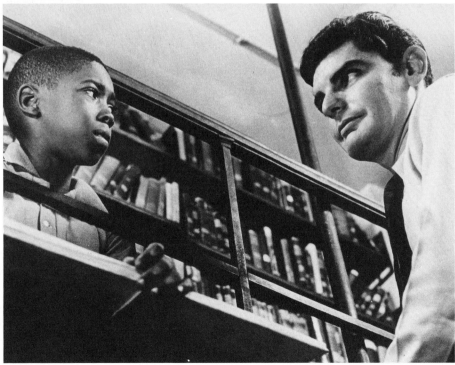

Goodbye Columbus In the 1969 movie version of Philip Roth's novella, Richard Benjamin plays the hero who works in the Newark Public Library. The youngster was drawn to the library for picture books with paintings by Gauguin. (MOMA Film Still Archives)

Restoration In 1968, the old Jefferson
Market Courthouse building in New
York City reopened as a branch library.
Saved from the threat of the wrecker's
ball, it was an example of adaptive use
that pleased historic preservationists.
Poet Marianne Moore was so taken with
the new library that she declared she
would do a great deal of her living at the
building known to many as "Old Jeff."
(New York Public Library, photo by
Sheldon Ramsdell)

The Old Central When these photographs were taken in the mid-1960s, the days of the old Central Public Library in Mount Vernon Square, in Washington, D.C., were numbered. It was built in 1903 and made possible with a gift of $250,000 from Andrew Carnegie. It was replaced in 1972 with the opening of the new Martin Luther King Memorial Library. The Washingtoniana room *(right)*, then as now, is a first-rate example of a local history room. (*The Washington Star, © The Washington Post*, reprinted by permission of the D.C. Public Library)

Glass Houses The Monessen Public Library in Monessen, Pennsylvania, was typical of the new, open libraries of the era. The new main building of the Minneapolis Public Library *(right and opposite below)*, which opened in 1961 was seen as a leading element in the rejuvenation of the Gateway area of that city. All across the country library architecture was changing dramatically from the classic to the modern. (ALA Archives and Minneapolis Public Library)

Sunday Patrons A busy Sunday afternoon at the Carnegie Library of Pittsburgh in 1963. Once the very idea of opening on the Sabbath was a matter of great controversy. In his essay on the subject, historian Sidney Ditzion said that it was an issue of such magnitude in nineteen-century Boston that it "split the whole number of Bostonians into two warring factions." (Carnegie Library of Pittsburgh)

URBAN
LIBRARIES
1969

The nation's public libraries have become a battleground in the war to make big cities livable.

Although only a few cities have gone through an emotional controversy over libraries similar to the disputes that have enveloped public schools all over the country, librarians have begun to admit that their turn-of-the-century buildings—with columns outside and "silence" signs inside—do not meet the needs of the large urban population that is poor, uneducated and unemployed.

The libraries are groping for new ways of reaching their new public. At the same time, they face demands from their traditional clients—educated, middle-class professionals—whose suburban libraries are too new to be comprehensive. These suburbanites account for a major portion of urban library service. Yet many prefer to buy a paperback rather than be 17th on the library's waiting list for the current best seller. The libraries must also satisfy business and industrial clients who remain in the cities.

Despite all of these demands, book circulation is going down in most big city libraries...

In some cities, the result has been a campaign by the libraries to justify their existence.

What the librarians call "outreach" has become the theme of a series of experiments in getting people and books and ideas together.

Many libraries have developed new versions of the traditional bookmobile. Now these libraries on wheels arrive with loudspeakers blaring rock music and set up shop on the sidewalk. In Newark, a storyteller who rides in the bookmobile attracts the neighborhood children as she sits under a beach umbrella on the street and reads aloud.

The Brooklyn Public Library has hired four "community coordinators" and "unleashed" them in various neighborhoods, librarian John Frantz says.

One of these is Frederick (Fritz) Johns, who roams the streets passing out books and setting up programs based on the library's materials.

Looking like a bald and beardless Santa Claus, Fritz arrived for lunch the other day with his arms full of shopping bags. "You wouldn't believe what I've been doing," he said. "Conducting a film program in a men's room."

A sports club in the Red Hook area of Brooklyn's docks had asked him to show a movie on the heritage of blacks in America. Since the only club facilities are a swimming pool and stadium, Johns showed the film in a combination men's room and locker room. He reported that his audience of about 80 youths didn't seem to mind, and that many left with books that he had brought along for them to look at.

Brooklyn pioneered the "3Bs" program, in which book collections are left in bars, beauty shops and barber shops for use by customers. It is a program that has become something of a symbol of "outreach" efforts to librarians and others who don't like them. These critics claim that the "3Bs" program is a splashy gimmick without substance.

But many libraries have picked up the idea of distributing inexpensive paperbacks and not worrying about whether they are returned, on the principle that their job is to make books easily available. . . .

—From the *Washington Post* (August 24, 1969) by Ellen Hoffman

Community Action The decade saw the emerging of the Great Society and the War on Poverty. Some of that money went into library programs, and such initiatives were deemed the "wave of the future" by many in the library profession. Great amounts of money were not forthcoming, but the early demonstration efforts did help get libraries deeper into the business of dealing with illiteracy and poverty. Depicted here is a story-telling program associated with a Baltimore Community Action Program in 1968. (Enoch Pratt Free Library)

Circulation Despite much talk about the automation of the public library, most systems chugged along exchanging books in the the pre-electronic manner. At the end of the decade, *Library Journal* called progress in this area "very thin," adding that "promises and projections are still being made." Two views *(below)* from the Carnegie Library of Pittsburgh are typical. (Carnegie Library of Pittsburgh)

Ashore and Afloat Military library services kept up with the times. Shown here are the library on the aircraft carrier USS *Independence (above);* ward service to patients at the U.S. Army Hospital at Fort Dix, New Jersey *(right);* and a librarian *(above right)* bringing books to troops during an exercise at the Yakima Firing Center, Yakima, Washington. (DAA, ALA Archives)

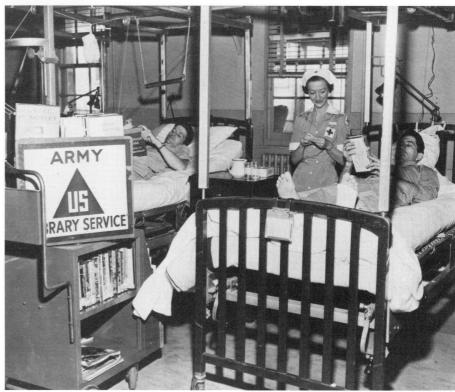

Model T A 1913 Ford *(opposite)* is squeezed into the main entrance of the Free Library of Philadelphia for a 1967 exhibit entitled "Cars of Yesteryear." Clearance was less than one inch. (Free Library of Philadelphia)

188

National Library Week—1969 The American Library Association has long used the most contemporary graphics to promote libraries in general and National Library Week in particular. The commissioned work has ended up on posters and bookmarks. Included here is a Peter Max poster *(opposite)*, which was very much of its time (1969), but which now has the look of a historical artifact. *(Library Journal)*

March on Washington Librarians
protesting the Vietnam War during the
November 1969 March on Washington.
This was not a "business as usual"
period for libraries and librarians.
Reporting on the previous year, *Library
Journal* said in its January 1, 1970, issue,
"The year 1969 has been one of the most
eventful for librarians, and it looks as
though many of the issues raised will
increase in importance in the next year
or two. If we could single out the topics
which caught the interest of librarians
most in the past year, they would lead
off with intellectual freedom, closely
followed by the insurgent groups within
library associations, groups which raise
the issue of social responsibility,
democracy within professional
associations, and Vietnam." (*Library
Journal,* photo by John Berry)

THE SEVENTIES
READ ON!

If any one factor dominated the world of the public library in the 1970s, it was economic. On one hand, libraries had all sorts of new ideas on their agendas—new "multimedia" services was a common one—but on the other hand, local, state, and Federal budgets were being cut back, and the allotments for public libraries were among the hardest hit. Add to this dramatically rising costs. In the 1975–76 period alone the average price of a hardcover book went from $14.09 to $16.19. By 1979 it had risen to $20.10. The mixture of deep cuts and soaring costs brought about a decade-long decline in the fortunes of the American public library.

In some areas the battle for the budget inflicted heavier damage than in others, as branches were closed and bookmobiles removed from service in addition to cuts in hours, services, and staff. Over the course of the decade, for ex-

EIGHT

ample, the District of Columbia public-library system dropped thirty percent of its staff, stopped its bookmobile service, and cut branch hours from an average of 72 hours a week to 40. This story was repeated in other cities, suburbs, and small towns. In 1977 the Fletcher Free Library in Burlington, Vermont, was faced with a budget that meant abolishing five staff positions, cutting hours by thirty percent, ending all telephone reference service, and eliminating all outreach programs.

Some libraries, such as Los Angeles, simply stopped buying books and some, such as New York City, were forced to put new books in warehouses when it was found there was no money to catalog and shelve them.

It seemed that that the rug was being pulled out from under the libraries again and again. In 1973, for instance, there had been 140 million Federal dollars appropriated for libraries, but when President Richard M. Nixon presented his fiscal 1974 budget, there was not a nickle allocated for libraries. In response to this deteriorating situation, on Tuesday, May 8, 1973, public libraries across America dimmed their lights to protest Federal cutbacks to libraries. A few relied on candlelight. "In our case it will be symbolic," said one small-town librarian, "because our lighting is so poor that you can't tell in the daytime whether they're on or not."

As if this were not enough, the decade witnessed a rising number of library thefts involving books, records, and other properties. Library security was becoming a major concern for administrators.

Libraries seemed to be on the ropes and while some eventually recovered better than others, serious damage had been inflicted. To this day many still suffer from staff and hours reductions first felt during that time.

Nonetheless, when the American Library Association reached its one-hundredth anniversary in 1976, it did have some reason to celebrate. Circulation had jumped ten percent from 1974 to 1975—the largest one-year jump since the statistics were first compiled 37 years earlier and, despite all the cutbacks and budgetary restraints, the American public library had somehow managed to develop some of those new, nontraditional "multimedia" offerings. It was becoming harder and harder to think of something that was *not* being offered at one or another library, whether it was pets, tools, toys, cassettes, audio tapes, exercise classes, rock concerts, musical instruments, or, in the case of the St. Louis Public Library, a hotline for fishing information. When the *Wall Street Journal* addressed this diversification in a 1975 article, it was entitled "With a Little Luck, You May Even Find Books in the Library."

Signs of the Times Two photographs capture some of the response to problems of the era. The first *(right)* survives without a caption but serves well as a generic image for the people in many communities fighting to save libraries. The second *(opposite)* is from a protest in 1969 in front of the Newark, New Jersey, City Hall against the closing of the city's Museum and Library. Such protests were not without effect. Patron complaints in Philadelphia helped get part of that city's library budget restored, and the Newark library did not close. In New York, a patron was so upset when he heard that his branch library in the Bronx was closing that he anted up $15,000 of his own money to keep it open until other volunteers succeeded in raising another $20,000. (*Library Journal*; second photo, New Jersey Newsphotos)

ANYBODY GOT FIFTEEN CENTS? 1970

On April 1 dawn came just as it had on every other day to the big ugly city nestled by the big ugly swamp. Four hundred thousand men and women and children got out of bed one way or another, shaved, showered, gulped their Wheaties, brushed their teeth, and hustled off to school and work and shopping centers exactly as they had on every other day. Outside Megapol in the suburbs four hundred thousand other people jammed the street cars and buses and automobiles and poured into the city exactly as they had on every other day.

Except that no one came to the Library. This was the day the Library was to close. Back in mid-February the Megapol City Council had decided that this was the only way they could cut the bankrupt city's tax rate by fifteen cents.

Could the Library really close? The President did not think so. He even issued a Proclamation: Libraries, he said, are arsenals of the accumulated knowledge and wisdom of mankind; indeed, by expanding the horizons of even one American, our libraries serve us all. . . .

The Governor issued a Proclamation: The State was overwhelmed by this impending tragedy. Megapol Public Library had long served not simply Megapol but the entire northern half of the State. Megapol Library had indeed been officially designated as the Metropolitan Reference Library for that half of the state. Megapol Library should have financial help from the State, but the Legislature (of the same political faith as the President) had refused to help. The Governor's appeals to the federal government for help had gone unanswered. But the Governor was convinced that the local government would surely be able to find some money somewhere; . . .

In middle March the City Council held a public meeting to consider the Library and the budget. Some four hundred people attended.

It was a stormy meeting. After four hours the Mayor's gavel brought it to a close and the Mayor made a statement:

"Last year the Library served over a million readers. But the town which owns that library has only 400,000 people. More than half are black and many live at a poverty or below-poverty level. Sixty percent of Megapol's land is untaxable. Four hundred thousand people—and only 400 of them here tonight! Why? Because they need something more than books. This city has some things it must do or it will simply fall apart. Fire, police, hospitals, schools; the budget takes care of these things—not as much as it should but as much as it can. The only other item in the budget is our anti-poverty program. Food, clothing, housing, job training; from which of these shall we take fifteen cents for the Library? These 400,000 are my people. I do not intend to neglect the basic needs of my people just so some guy fifty miles away can find out about Alaska's fishing. The Library building is sound; the books are all there. Both will keep till we have enough money to open them again."

On April 1 dusk came just as it had on every other day to the big ugly city nestled by the big ugly swamp. Four hundred thousand people hustled off home exactly as they had on every other day. Four hundred thousand other people jammed the street cars and buses and automobiles and poured out of the city just as they had on every other day.

Except that no one came out of the Library.

—From *Tales of Melvil's Mouser or Much Ado About Libraries*, by Paul Dunkin (R. R. Bowker Co., 1970)

Rolling Stock If many localities were forced to cut their bookmobile fleets in the 1970s, some were able to put new ones on the streets. This special Denver Public Library vehicle *(above)* was aimed at the needs of the elderly who found it inconvenient or impossible to visit the library. (Denver Public Library)

Reading Room Afloat The newly opened library aboard the aircraft carrier USS *John F. Kennedy.* The completely soundproofed library is on the third deck adjacent to the crew's lounge. The photograph was taken in 1971, when there was a certain irony in the contrast between this new seagoing library and the problems with the old libraries ashore. (DAA)

Fisheye View This 1971 photograph of the Main Reading Room of the Library of Congress by Ainsworth Johnson has become something of a classic. It shows the room in all its glory from floor to dome. The Library of Congress did not suffer during the 1970s but rather expanded in many directions, including the addition of the new $160 million Madison Building. (Library of Congress)

New Librarian Daniel Boorstin *(right)* became the Librarian of Congress in 1975 after a long career as historian, writer, and educator. As the twelfth Librarian he has made his mark on the place in many ways, ranging from the establishment of the Center for the Book, an organization set up to encourage reading, to the installation of picnic tables on the Neptune Plaza. (Library of Congress)

PLEASE POST AND/OR PUBLISH

**JOIN THE NATIONAL TASK FORCE
TO FUND AND STAFF THE WOMEN'S HISTORY LIBRARY**

We at the Women's History Library need you to make our irreplaceable material on women available to you and everyone. Dedicated, long-term volunteers are needed to continue our microfilming project. By making our entire collection available in microfilm copies to local libraries and women's resource centers, thousands of people will be able to use its invaluable resources for research and education. With your help, we can make a reality of our dream of microfilming *all* our material for nationwide use.

Because all available staff time must be devoted to this project, the Library cannot be open to those doing research (unfortunately, we have never received funding for regular staff).

THE PROJECT

WORK INVOLVES: Corresponding with women's periodicals; inventorying and filing into 2,000 topical research files of newspaper clippings, research papers, poetry, and graphics; cutting, classifying, cataloging and filing women's newsletters, journals and newspaper clippings. The work is exacting, as the material will be prepared for microfilming and must be "camera ready."

Some of the specific areas include our material about: :

Black women	Women and film
Soviet women	Women and health
Women's studies	Women and law

A NOTE ON WORKING CONDITIONS: The work is routine, but the diversity of the people and the material makes the difference. Due to lack of any public funding, the Library is still located in the home of its founder, so work space is limited. Be prepared for second-hand equipment and donated supplies (bring more!). Part-time volunteer office workers are also needed. Hours vary: days — nights — weekends — but must be at least ten hours a week for office and library workers.

WHY WE NEED YOU

The Women's History Library has been staffed by college work-study students; 80% of their wages are paid to them by the Federal Government, the other 20% is provided by personal donations to us and royalties from the sale of our original women's periodicals collection on microfilm. (Available through Bell & Howell in Wooster, Ohio, this microfilm is now being used in 60 college, high school and public libraries.) We will market future microfilms, however.

As you know, funds for Federal Work-Study programs are being cut off in many colleges, so we must change to a basically volunteer staff to continue this vital project.

All material in our International Women's History Archive by and about the current women's movement has been donated by member individuals and organizations. By putting the complete collection on microfilm, you will be helping them to publicize their efforts and ideas.

Please call first. Ask for Laurel, Katy or Laura.

**WOMEN'S HISTORY RESEARCH CENTER, INC.
2325 Oak Street, Berkeley, California 94708
(415) 524-7772**

New Concerns This undated and self-explanatory handbill from the files of *Library Journal* reflected the growing interest in feminism among librarians and patrons. *(Library Journal)*

WHEN READERS BECOME SUSPECTS 1970

The federal government, through the Treasury Department, has begun a systematic effort to obtain the names of people who check library materials about explosives and, in some cases, books loosely described as "subversive" or "militant."

Investigators of the Treasury's Internal Revenue Service have been quietly visiting libraries for at least two months seeking the information. The result is believed to be the nation's first coordinated effort to gather intelligence information that makes Americans suspect because of what they read.

Numerous librarians and officials of the American Library Association, questioned during the past few days about the Treasury agents' visits, confirm that the investigators have sought the titles and the names of borrowers of books listed under the heading "Explosives" in library catalogues and, in some cases, titles suggesting contents related to guerrilla warfare. Beyond that, in at least one library system an agent simply requested that the librarian provide the names of people who have checked out "militant or subversive" books. When she refused, the investigator angrily lectured her on refusing to cooperate with the government.

The federal agents in some cases, upon meeting resistance by librarians, have suggested that they might obtain subpoenas for the information, which presumably would place the burden upon the librarians themselves to laboriously extract the desired information from microfilmed records. And in another case the agents, after a refusal from a librarian, contacted the city attorney's office, which opened the library files by advising the librarian in writing that, contrary to library tradition, all library records were public information.

Inquiries for this report have revealed that the agents' activities are not simply localized, pertaining to specific investigations, but part of a nationwide campaign to gather the names of readers of certain kinds of books. . . .

It has now been confirmed that the IRS is gathering the information nationally, through its Alcohol, Tobacco and Firearms Division, under a very broad construal of IRS enforcement powers authorized by the Gun Control Act of 1968. That act defines destructive devices (including explosives, mines, missiles and poison gas) and provides that anyone manufacturing them must file an application with the Secretary of the Treasury and purchase a tax stamp.

Librarians are uncertain about what is done with the names of readers once the IRS has obtained them. In recent weeks, Sen. Sam J. Ervin Jr. of North Carolina, chairman of the Senate Subcommittee on Constitutional Rights, has charged that the use of government computers to amass files on suspect citizens is in itself a threat to Americans' freedoms.

When asked whether agents have been gathering names of book borrowers, Harold Serr, director of the IRS Alcohol, Tobacco and Firearms Division, said: "I wouldn't swear that they haven't, because when you are looking for information you go wherever you can find it. But unless they are working on a particular person, I don't think it would be worthwhile to find information that way." Although his office has not specifically directed investigators to gather names of book borrowers, he said, "it's possible that some investigator is looking for this." . . .

—From *South Today* (July 9, 1970), by Reese Cleghorn

After Mencken Actor David Wayne *(right)* star of the one-man show "An Unpleasant Evening with H. L. Mencken," which premiered in 1972, visits the H. L. Mencken Room at the Enoch Pratt. (Enoch Pratt Free Library)

Stars on the Steps Robert Redford and Dustin Hoffman *(opposite above)* as Bob Woodward and Carl Bernstein in *All the President's Men,* shown on the steps of the Library of Congress. In the book and in the 1976 Warner Brothers film the two reporters with the aid of a clerk are able to go through records of the Library to see what books had been taken out by the Nixon White House. The Library steadfastly maintained that all such records were and are confidential. In another movie of the period, which was originally called *The Senator* but was released as *The Seduction of Joe Tynan,* a scene being shot in the Library ended abruptly when a technician crashed through a ceiling and landed on a desk. The film crew was banished. (MOMA Film Still Archives)

Bicentennial Library The East Shore Area Branch Library of the Dauphin County Pennsylvania Library System *(right)* opened in 1976. Other setbacks aside, many systems continued to grow during the period. (Dauphin County Library System)

1970s Nostalgia What would a collection of photos about the decade be without one of a streaker? This one *(opposite bottom)* appears to have been working to promote libraries. *(Library Journal,* photo by Lloyd Moebius of the *Flint Journal)*

THE DEWEY–CASANOVA SYNDROME 1976

. . . Melvil Dewey, one of the founders of the American Library Association, originated the Dewey Decimal System, still in use in the libraries of 123 countries today. Of all human librarians Dewey is the one most likely to be mistaken for a computer. As a child in school in Adams Center, N.Y. in the 1850's, "he could work a problem in arithmetic in his head quicker than the others could on paper," his teacher recalled later. "Another characteristic was his mania for system and classification," she added. "It was his delight to arrange his mother's pantry, systematizing and classifying its contents."

Dewey's lifelong enemy was disorder, and his passion was for saving time. His fervor . . . led not only to his lasting library contributions but also propelled him to the forefront of other reforms dear to the heart of the completely rational—notably phonetic spelling and what he called "the metrik sistem of weits & mezures." . . .

Dewey's orthography probably pushed rationality farther than it was meant to go. "The English languaj," he wrote, "is the most illojical, unsyentific, unskolarly and altogether worst speling of ani languaj in the world. . . . It addlez peopl's brainz," he said. Upon leaving home, Dewey shortened his name from Melville Louis Kossuth Dewey to plain Melvil Dewey. Then, never one to do things by halves, he began signing his name "Mel Dui."

Casanova—*that* Casanova—was something else. In 1785, at 60, down on his luck, the great days behind him, gouty, a wig on his bony head and his mouth full of china teeth, the legendary adventurer was rescued by a young friend, patron and sport named Count Waldstein, who owned Waldstein Castle, a magnificent pile at Dux in Bohemia. Here he installed Casanova as librarian. The pay was 1,000 florins a year, and a horse and carriage.

Here Casanova spent the last 13 years of his life. They were, in large part, dismal years, certainly anticlimactic, but good things came of them. He read everything, corresponded widely, regaled visitors with gaudy lies and gamy truths, occasionally argued literature and philosophy with the likes of Goethe and Schiller, kicked the servants in the shins, and, most satisfyingly, wrote constantly on his memoirs, which would be published in 12 volumes 30 years after his death.

Most librarians today are neither Deweys nor Casanovas. As a group they are knowledgeable, well-trained in their art. They carry degrees in something called library science, but they practice an art, or ply a craft, of finding what people want, often before people know they want it.

Best of all, they are human. Only the Luddites among them would *close* the library to the computer—especially when that computer can perform quickly the necessary, but less human, jobs: the tedious chores and searches essential to keep the various publics informed—at a price that leaves enough money in the budget to continue to buy books.

But a computer is not a librarian. As one great librarian, Lawrence Clark Powell, wrote a few years back, "A good librarian is not a social scientist, a documentalist, a retrievalist, or an automaton. A good librarian is a librarian: a person with good health and warm heart, trained by study and seasoned by experience to catalyze books and people."

—From *The New York Times Magazine* (October 17, 1976), by Patrick Butler

Boosters Streamers and posters of the decade promoting Children's Book Week, National Library Week, and libraries in general. (*Library Journal* and ALA)

READ-IN '71

READ-IN '71

READ-IN '71

Books for all reasons

PHOTO BY TANA HOBAN

207

At the very end of the decade, November 1979, the White House held a Conference on Library and Information Science. More than 2,000 attended. According to news accounts from the conference, it was an odd mix of two trends. One was the reality of the decade-long downward spiral that kept the delegates preoccupied with the issue of basic funding. The other was the promise of high technology that was seen as the bridge to the library of the future. It seemed as though we were moving toward a high-tech, real-time, state-of-the-art library but which would only be open thirty hours a week, would be closed on weekends, and could scarcely afford new books. All the computers and information systems on display at the Conference did not overcome the fact that libraries were not getting the support they needed. As one delegate was quoted in the *Washington Post*, "Libraries are plagued by the image that we are nice but not essential. It plagues us at budget time that we are icing on the cake, not meat and potatoes."

First Reader President Carter spoke warmly about books and libraries at the Conference and ended by telling the delegates, "You've got a friend in the White House." (National Commission on Libraries and Information Science)

At the Conference The Youth Caucus is interviewed *(above)* as a group, and Ralph Nader *(right)* is shown after his address to the delegates. Several years earlier, Nader had reacted to the closing of branch libraries in New York City with this comment, which applied to many communities: "Over history's time, the destruction of libraries, whether by war or dictatorship, has been viewed as a serious blow to freedom and democracy. In New York, it's seen merely as a way to save some money." (NCLIS)

SERVICE
AND
CYBERNETICS

Public libraries came out of the 1970s in a collective daze as a host of elements, from domestic inflation to a foreign-oil embargo, had seemingly conspired to work against them. Murphy's Law had ruled.

There was to be no dramatic, overnight turnaround. The decline of libraries was halted in most locales and, as inflation subsided, gradual advances were made. Some have been winning back their losses by adding a few staff positions here and a few operating hours there. Annual reports from individual systems have been speaking in terms of "renewed commitment."

Libraries were learning that Federal aid was not going to be anything more than an irregular, small, but important element of their working budgets. Local funds were still the overwhelming source of fuel for the public library as these 1982 figures show:

NINE

Source	Approximate Percentage
Local	79.2
Other	9.3
State	7.7
Federal	3.7

Libraries were learning to fight for every nickle, whether it be through the budgetary processes of local government or from outside sources. This ranged from major fundraising drives involving individual and corporate givers to such grassroots standbys as car washes, cake sales, and used-book sales. In Pawtucket, Rhode Island, they have been staging "celebrity shoe auctions"; in Brooklyn residents are being encouraged to contribute to the "Buy a Book for Brooklyn" campaign. Unusual alliances often produced remarkable results. In 1983 the main New York Public Library, which had been forced to close on Thursdays since 1975, was able to reopen on Thursdays thanks to private gifts from Barbara Tuchman and the Chase Manhattan Bank. More and more libraries were planning and hoping for greater involvement by the private sector in their futures.

As automation really began to take root in the 1980s, the computer was seen as a force for greater productivity and economic efficiency, rather than as a spellbinding "marvel of the future." Card catalogs were beginning to give way to terminals, microfilm readers, and dictionary-sized binders of printout. The road to automation was often a rocky one aggravated by those—patrons and staff alike—who felt a library was not meant to operate on "downtime."

Lest anyone think that the future was all blue skies, in 1986 the Library of Congress was forced to make cutbacks. This library, which had never been subject to the problems plaguing local public libraries, had been caught in the sudden ax swing of the Gramm–Rudman Budget Reduction Act. Hours were cut by a third, staff by 300, and the working budget by $18.3 million. As this is being written, protesters are holding a vigil in front of the Library. Even if some of the cuts are eventually restored, the image of a hamstrung Library of Congress underscores the point that in the late twentieth century libraries of all sizes are highly vulnerable public institutions.

Traditions The Main Reading Room *(above)* and the massive card catalog at the main New York Public Library *(right)*. The old oaken card catalog was officially closed in 1985, but the main reading room has been restored and its original glory survives. (New York Public Library, photos © Anne Day)

Shift in Progress The Library of Congress is now being called the most technologically sophisticated repository of knowledge in the world. This is being achieved with some major changes including the abandonment of the old road map to the place, the card catalog system. Shown: a man working in the old-fashioned manner *(far left)*, juxtaposed with one of the new terminals. (NCLIS, photo by Chad Evans Wyatt, and Library of Congress)

Public Catalog Room Now this room boasts thirty catalog terminals. The catalog is now known as CATNYP (for *CAT*alog of the *New York Public* library). The long oak tables and their bronze lamps have been refinished. Alfred Kazin wrote of those tables in his book *New York Jew:* "Year after year I seemed to have nothing more delightful to do than to sit much of the day and many an evening at one of those great golden tables acquainting myself with every side of my subject." (NYPL, photo by Scott McKiernan)

Contrast New York's old and new systems shown side by side. Commenting on the shift, NYPL President Vartan Gregorian said, "This leap into the 21st century of 19th-century-style surroundings." (NYPL, Scott McKiernan and Anne Day)

Philadelphia Moving quickly into the new era, the Free Library of Philadelphia has installed a system featuring touch-sensitive screens. Touch the screen and find a book, touch it again and find out if it has been checked out, another touch tells you when it is due back. Here we see one *(top right)* of the new screens, which have been installed in all of the branches as well as in the main library, and Director Keith Doms *(above)*, who is leading the system into the future. (Free Library of Philadelphia)

Maggie's Place Named for a retired librarian, Maggie's Place is the pride of the Pikes Peak Library District of Colorado Springs. It has achieved a national reputation as one of the most advanced systems of its kind. Its handlers brag that it is up and running 99.9 percent of the time and it gives out all sorts of information up to and including ski conditions, car-pool information, and day-care availability. (Pikes Peak Library District)

Back on the Street The District of Columbia's first bookmobile for the elderly is equipped with a wheelchair lift. Besides books, it offers film programs, storytelling and book discussions. Such services were giving the bookmobile a boost after suffering the setback of the energy crisis. (DCPL, photo by H. Greene)

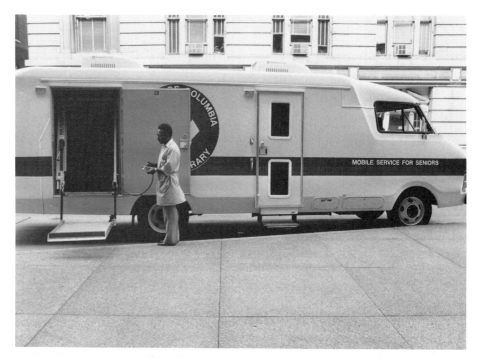

Book Brigade Scenes like this have become common when smaller libraries move from old to new quarters. Residents are mobilized to carry the books from one building to another. The move depicted here took place in Chestertown, Maryland, at the Kent County Public Library. (Kent County Public Library)

LIBRARY VERSE 1980s

FROM THE LIBRARY

Our annual report
To the heads of the Town:
Circulation is up.
Computer is down.

A PLEA TO THE CHILDREN'S LIBRARIAN

Don't computerize your catalogue.
Don't tamper with each tray.
Don't let the spindles dwindle.
Don't cart the cards away.

I know that, with computers,
Subject search becomes a game
At which five-year-olds are expert
And four-year-olds the same.

But I can't calmly contemplate
The tumult in the town
When the kids commence complaining
That the catalogue is down.

So don't let the labels languish.
Don't tell the tabs they're through.
What was good enough for Dewey
Should be good enough for you.

TAKE A LIBRARIAN TO LUNCH

Take a Librarian to lunch.
You know that she deserves it.
Ascertain her favorite food,
Then find a place that serves it.

Seek out, too, an ambience
That you are sure will suit her:
Some place that bans all little kids
And where there's no computer.

Serve her with her favorite drink:
Champagne? Or something diet?
And make it clear that, at this meal,
There are no rules on quiet.

Ask her to tell you of her job:
Which books are circulating?
Which patron said what funny thing?
You'll find it fascinating.

But do leave promptly when you've shared
Good talk and drink and food.
Librarians must be back when due
And may not be renewed.*

*N.B. Nothing here should be construed as precluding the taking of a male Librarian to lunch.

——By Pyke Johnson, Jr.; poems originally appeared in *Connecticut Libraries*.

Award Winner This Thousand Oaks, California, public library serves as a prime example of the often daring library architecture of the 1980s. This one won a joint award from the American Institute of Architects and the American Library Association in 1983. *(Library Journal)*

Los Angeles: Down But Not Out Not only did the Los Angeles Public Library suffer from the same economic problems as the rest of the nation, but it was also hit with particularly severe cutbacks as the result of Proposition 13 and other statewide tax limitations. Despite deep cuts and dislocation, the system has been able to retain its vitality and provide for the diverse neighborhoods it serves through its branches. Evidence: the new San Pedro Regional Branch Library *(right)*, which came into being in 1983; the Chinatown library *(center bottom)*, which was restored and expanded in the same year; and *(far right)* the interior of the Central Library, which was undergoing a major expansion when hit by a devastating fire in April 1986. (Los Angeles Public Library)

218

Children's Library The Noyes Library in Kensington, Maryland, is part of the large Montgomery County Department of Public Libraries. The building *(top left)* is the oldest standing library building in the surrounding Washington, D.C., metropolitan area, and the area's only library exclusively devoted to children. Shown as it looks today, it is one of many reminders that historic preservation and modern librarianship can be a potent combination. It predates the main Library of Congress building by four years. Because the *y* in Noyes is capitalized on the edifice, some of its young patrons call it the "No-Yes" Library, while others enjoy the play on "noise" or "noise-Y". (Montgomery County Department of Public Libraries, photo by Joe Neil)

Branches In many cities the branch libraries were particularly hard hit by cutbacks. New York's were among the hardest hit, with staff slashed by a third and hours cut in half. Recovery has been slow but sure. Scenes in New York Public Library Branches—the Donnell Library Center, the Castle Hill Branch *(opposite below: left and right)*, and the Chatham Square Branch *(top right)*—hint at their importance. (NYPL, first photo © Anne Day)

Video High Jinks The head of the Dauphin County, Pennsylvania, Library System audio-visual department, Edward Cool, dons his Capt. Video togs to promote the new video-cassette rental service. (Dauphin County Library System)

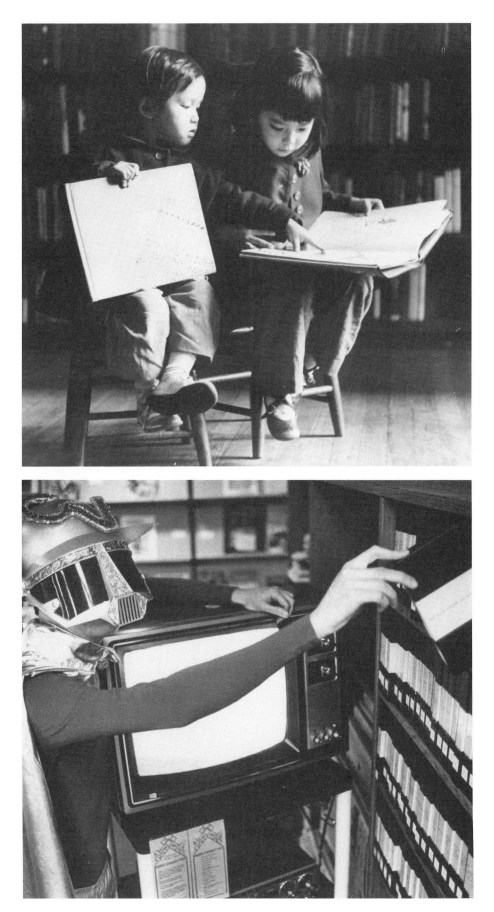

THE UNIVERSAL LIBRARY CARD 1985

The Elkhart Public Library in Indiana, like some of its counterparts around the country, marked off the second week in September for discussions and films connected with "Banned Books Week." A local television news personality thought this meant the library was celebrating the banning of books and asked for a list of titles the staff considered harmful.

A barely patient librarian explained that the intent of the week was to celebrate resistance to censorship during a decade when more and more books are being challenged in public libraries and schools. One title rising higher and higher on the national hit list, by the way, is *The Diary of Anne Frank.* The complaint cards talk about its "sexuality.". . .

The director of the Elkhart Public Library, George Brich, somewhat resembles Sydney Greenstreet in size, bearing and astuteness. I asked him if the library, like others around the country, had been under siege more often than usual in the past year.

"Not really," the library director said. "We have the complaint forms and the review committees and all that, so they know what procedures to follow. But actually, if you listen to them when they come in to complain—really listen—often that's all they want. Not long ago, a Baptist minister stormed into the library. Some books had set him off. I took him into my office and we talked for two hours. About all sorts of things. He was a lot quieter when he left. And I said to him, 'Reverend, my door is always open.' And he said, 'So is mine.' "

Brich allowed himself a brief retrospective smile. "I tell my staff, 'Listen to them! Not condescendingly, but with empathy.' The people who come in with complaints feel very deeply about what troubles them. They need to express themselves. It's like writing a letter to the paper. If the paper prints it, you feel better."

In the Elkhart library, as in a large number of public libraries around the country, children are not restricted to children's sections. With what Brich calls The Universal Library Card in use, kids can take out any book they want, and any number of books they want. In my time, kids were supposed to stay in their place in the library. And we could take out only two books at a time. I figured they were worried that our eyes might wear out.

Now, with kids free to check out any book, I wonder if the library often hears from parents alarmed at what their tykes have brought in the door. "Oh, sometimes a parent will get angry at a book a kid has brought home," Brich said. "And the parent will bring in the kid's card and tell us he's returning it. We mail the card back to the child. It's his card. The child can return it, but no one can return it for the child." . . .

—From *The Washington Post,* September 21, 1985, by Nat Hentoff.

Ghostbusters. Venkman (Bill Murray), Stantz (Dan Ackroyd), and Spengler (Harold Ramis) confront an unfriendly spirit in the stacks of the New York Public Library in the 1984 box-office hit.

Copyright © 1984, Columbia Pictures Industries, Inc., All Rights Reserved.

Freedom Fighter Former Library Commissioner Amanda S. Rudd of the Chicago Public Library congratulates novelist Kurt Vonnegut on being one of the first winners of the Freedom to Read Award in 1983. The award is cosponsored by the Friends of the Chicago Public Library and Playboy Enterprises. Concern over censorship is not misplaced as the number of efforts to get books taken out of libraries tripled between 1981 and 1983. (Chicago Public Library)

Time of Forgiveness Libraries have gone to extremes to get their books back. In this picture taken in 1983 a major Forgiveness Week was in effect at the Free Library of Philadelphia. Here we see library staff members take in the overdues. In this particular effort the results were dramatic, with close to 35,000 people bringing back more than 150,000 books—one borrowed in 1922! Other libraries have used other techniques to get borrowers to bring books back. One of the more unusual was the Caroll County, Maryland, system, which offered coupons for a free order of french fries at a local fast food outlet for anyone bringing back two overdue books. (Free Library of Philadelphia, photos by Prentice Cole and Ron Williams)

On Line Some library computer systems have gotten beyond the housekeeping chores associated with inventory and circulation, and have become sources of useful information. The Job and Career Information Center at the Enoch Pratt *(center)* is a case in point as is the anSir Information and Referral Service *(right)* operating in 160 West Virginia libraries. (NCLIS, photos from Enoch Pratt, David V. Tirschman, and West Virginia Library Commission, photo by Ross Taylor)

224

Congressional Recollections Ceremony *(opposite top right)* in which Former Members of Congress (FMC) present the Librarian of Congress with a collection of oral histories created by that group. The Bicentennial era sparked an interest in oral history that benefitted many libraries, which have now become repositories for those collections. (Library of Congress)

Local Hero The young man shown here *(right)* with his father is Jason Hardman. He is testifying at a 1982 joint Congressional hearing on the information needs of rural America. Young Hardman was growing up in Elsinore, Utah, where there was no library. The remnants of an old library were packed away, and he persisted in getting local authorities to let him open one. He helped bring attention to the plight of small-town and rural libraries. "Soon enough," wrote columnist Colman McCarthy in the *Washington Post*, "Jason will be demanding on-line data bases and videotext systems for his library. He deserves to have them, if we want him to be a knowing citizen." (NCLIS, photo by Karen Keeney)

Muralists Members of three Philadelphia street gangs were recruited to paint murals on the graffiti-covered walls of the Cobbs Creek Branch Library in West Philadelphia. Two local artists, who supervised the work, are shown with the young men who did the painting. (Free Library of Philadelphia, photos by Norman Y. Lono and Sam Psoras, Philadelphia *Daily News*)

As special collections have grown, libraries have become centers for major exhibitions and programs to show them off. Commenting on the trend toward major, thematic shows in public libraries, *Museum News* said in 1985 that "it indicates a move to restore libraries to their former position as centers of public learning and cultural activities."

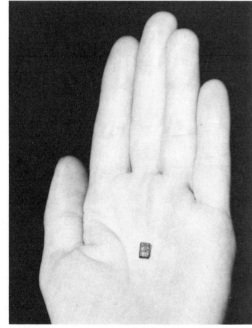

Compact Collection One of the smallest of 1,700 miniature books in a special collection at the Library of Congress *(above)*. The smallest book in the Library—and in the world—is titled *Ant* and is the size of an ant, 1.4 millimeters square. *Ant* is just one of the interesting and unusual items in the Library of Congress. To name a few others: Charles Dickens' walking stick, Houdini's scrapbooks, Alexander Graham Bell's first drawing of the telephone, and the world's first cookbook. (Library of Congress)

Black Cowboys This photograph of Bob Pickett was among a hundred rare images in a 1985 show, "The Black West," at the Schomburg Center for Research in Black Culture of the New York Public Library. (NYPL)

Diverse Holdings A sampling from the political memorabilia collection of the New York Public Library *(top right)* and an *Elvis Presley Scrapbook* by Joni Mabe, with pop-up pages edged in pink lace, from an exhibit on book arts. (NYPL, first photo by Anne Day)

Major Find Holding one of the greatest of all collections relating to Herman Melville, this trove of original material was acquired by the library in 1983. Shown are a fragment of the first draft of *Typee* and family letters. (NYPL, photo by Bob Serating)

FIRE
REMINISCENT
OF THE
DARK AGES
1982

Maybe there wasn't any point in it, but I drove over to Hollywood the other morning to see what was left of the branch library. . . .

Anyway, the Hollywood branch of the Los Angeles Public Library was hardly to be compared with the famous Library of Alexandria, whose fabulous collection preserved the learning and philosophy of the ancients and lighted the world for centuries. When the Library of Alexandria was destroyed that light went out, and perhaps it is not too fanciful to say that the resulting darkness was what made the Dark Ages dark. . . .

Yet the Hollywood branch, though it contained nothing as precious as the original manuscripts of Sophocles, Aeschylus and Euripides, as the Library of Alexandria did, was also a source of light, because it was connected, as a leaf is to the roots of a tree, to the great libraries of our own time.

Will Durant lived in one of those roomy old Spanish-style houses in the Hollywood hills just above Hollywood and Vine, and it was through that little branch just down the street from there that he and his wife, Ariel, did most of the research for their 13-volume "Story of Civilization." . . .

I had the good fortune some years ago to talk with the Durants in their home. Will was 90 then, and had given up the daily climb to his library upstairs; but Ariel led me up to the large bedroom whose walls were covered with books on western civilization.

As extensive as this private library was, though, it was far from adequate to their enormous task. Before he set out to the actual writing of each volume, the two of them read some 200 books, and most of those they obtained through the Hollywood branch library. . . .

As a young man, Will virtually lived in the New York City Public Library, but in pursuing his *magnum opus* here, in our so-called cultural wasteland, he showed that a library doesn't have to be the New York City Public Library or the Library of the British Museum and have stone lions couchant out in front of it to be of service to mankind.

In "Caesar and Christ" he dwelt on the destruction of the Alexandria library. . . .

A large part of the library, he noted, had already been destroyed "by Christian ardor," and the remainder had suffered such hostility and neglect that by the year 641, when Amr seized the great Egyptian city, there was little left to burn.

Looking at the blackened shell of the Hollywood branch that morning I naturally felt anger and revulsion. Such vandalism is sickening. But also, I realized, it was meaningless. The library had not been destroyed as an act of anti-intellectualism, or bigotry, but just because it happened to have been broken into by a couple of Neanderthal throwbacks who liked to play with matches.

I hope they catch the morons and put them away for a while in a place where they have nothing to burn but their own bedrolls, but that won't remove a far greater threat to our libraries.

An act of vandalism, a fire now and then, is a tragedy, but we aren't going to lose much ground to cavemen. It's the censors we have to watch out for, and they are creeping back into the circle of our campfires.

It was censorship, not fire, that destroyed the Library of Alexandria, and it can destroy ours.

—From the *Los Angeles Times* (April 21, 1982), by Jack Smith

Arson and Aftermath In April of 1982 an arsonist set fire to a pile of books in the 40-year old Art Deco-style Hollywood Library. The loss to this branch of the Los Angeles Public Library system was not only the building and most of its books but also rare memorabilia associated with the motion-picture business including, for instance, more than 7,000 original scripts. By the end of the year, however, the community was bringing the library back. The Samuel Goldwyn Foundation presented $2 million to rebuild it, the largest gift ever given to a California public library. Others contributing to the effort included Johnny Carson and the late Orson Welles. In addition to the destroyed library *(right),* we see Samuel Goldwyn Jr. *(below left)* presenting plans for the new building as the wrecker's ball hangs over the shell of the old one. Danny Thomas *(below right)* visits the warehouse where books for the new library are being processed. (Los Angeles Public Library)

230

THE LIBRARY IN TWO COUNTRIES 1985

The nicely dressed young woman, arms filled with books, crosses the border into the United States.

Moments later and without notifying authorities, she crosses back into Canada carrying a pile of documents.

And while the Customs officers of both countries have been aware of her presence in the area and cameras and border patrols are constantly on guard, she has traversed the international line hundreds of times a day for the last three years without being stopped.

This has all of the trappings of an intriguing international drama. But 24-year-old Kim Prangley is not a character in a spy thriller, though as head librarian of the Haskell Free Library, which straddles the border separating the two countries, she may be able to find such works of fiction on the bookshelves.

Through a special arrangement between the Canadian and American governments, residents from the surrounding communities are not required to report to Customs when they use the facilities. This is but one of the idiosyncrasies of the 80-year-old granite and buff brick building. An oddity set both in Derby Line, Vt., and Rock Island, Quebec, it has been the site of drug and smuggling trials, a passageway to freedom and a near appearance by the Beatles.

The visitor to the first-floor library must be prepared for an unique international journey, walking through the front door in the United States, proceeding to the book stacks or the children's room in Canada and back to the United States to sit in the reading room or to pick up the latest French- or English-language periodical. When a reader wishes to check out a book, the librarian, a Canadian resident who happens to have a dual citizenship, must leave her office in the Green Mountain State to step up to the dark oak lending desk in "La Belle Province.". . .

And though this structure, the only public building in the area set on the border (two-fifths in the United States and three-fifths in Canada), has earned a spot in "Ripley's Believe It Or Not!" and has been placed on the National Register of Historic Places, the residents of the border communities are typically reserved about the structure.

"I think that everyone that lives around here is well adjusted to it and they are used to it," said Prangley. "But everyone is very proud of it.". . .

A gift to the border communities from the Haskells, a prominent Derby Line family whose name is chiseled in granite over the front door, the grey edifice was deliberately situated on the border with the stipulation that area residents of both nations be forever *free* to use the facilities without encumbrances.

Walking through its interior, one senses a bygone era of horse and buggy and small, close-knit towns. The library is a striking example of Victorian decor and workmanship, complete with high tin ceilings, tiled marble fireplaces, stained glass windows and paneling—each room in a different native wood.

—From *BitterSweet* (April 1985), by Mark Lombard

High Rise The 14-story National Agricultural Library in Beltsville, Maryland *(opposite top)*, is the world's largest. It is a great national resource that many feel is not as well known as it should be. Besides the library itself, these pictures *(opposite)* show patrons being helped at the reference desk *(left)* and a man examining books in the library's Rare Books Reading Room *(right)* whose holdings include books published as early as the fifteenth century. (U.S. Department of Agriculture)

231

Familiar Faces One can visit virtually any size American library and the odds favor finding at least one colorful poster promoting libraries and reading. A small sampling of the posters that appear in the 1986 American Library Association Graphics Catalog. A large number feature well-known faces, whether from history, the funny papers, or Hollywood. Besides those seen here, other contemporary posters feature actress Goldie Hawn, boxer Sugar Ray Leonard, business leader Lee Iacocca, Mickey Mouse, and comedian George Burns. (ALA)

Orlando The newly expanded Orlando Public Library of the Orange County Library System takes up a full city block. The work was supported by a $22 million bond issue approved by local voters. (Orange County Library System)

Lions Restoration and renovation have become bywords for many libraries in the 1980s. One of the smaller tasks in the massive $45 million restoration of the New York Public Library was cleaning the lions *(right)*. The man who is credited with accelerating the rebirth of that system is Vartan Gregorian *(opposite bottom left)*, who became its president in 1981. (NYPL, first photo by Scott McKiernan)

Show Biz Mayor Koch *(opposite, far right)* of New York City singing with other members of the All-City Chorus outside the 42nd Street landmark at the 1983 opening of the ETC (Education, Theater and Culture) Center. (NYPL)

235

AFTERWORD
FOR ALL
CITIZENS
1984

Libraries remain the meccas of self-help, the most open of open universities . . . where there are no entrance examinations and no diplomas, and where one can enter at any age.

Daniel J. Boorstin,
Librarian of Congress

The recommendations of this report aim to foster the view that American libraries are congenial homes of ideas, homes to be enjoyed, valued, and used regularly by all Americans as they participate in the Learning Society. They may have to be redesigned to suit a new era, but the warmth, the concern, the help, the wealth of information remembered from previous visits still remain.

As citizens of the world's longest-lasting democracy, we *must* have easy access to libraries more than ever before. How well we govern, how intelligently we think through one difficult issue after another, how rationally we perform at center stage on the planet, will depend on our taking advantage of that resource.

Throughout our lives, the richest gold mines, the ones offering us the best chance to pan for the facts that yield knowledge, are libraries. Knowledge gained there can convert bias into understanding, and understanding into wisdom.

For decades, libraries have graced different sites in our town. But many of us have never bothered to pay attention to them. The public library, the school library media center, the academic and special libraries—all too often they are unknown quantities to us.

The time has come to change all that. Too much critical information is reverberating through our lives for us to continue ignoring those institutions. If they had to be shut for lack of support, we could wind up paying a fee to access a commercial data base through our home computer or searching for alternative sources of information, which would most likely be much more costly or inconvenient. Many of us probably could not afford that. As a result, the ideal of a democracy of ideas would evaporate, and information illiteracy would soar.

Fortunately, we do not have to design and build a new home for ideas from the ground up. It's already there. Libraries may need better furnishings, or more highly trained staff, or enhanced resources, or stronger links with neighbors, but the house stands. . . .

For the curious, for those with active and inquiring minds, libraries are a most welcome home. We have no institutions that are more likely components of a Learning Society spanning all our years; without them, a full Learning Society simply could not be realized.

Our nation should use the institutions it has. It should insist that our libraries—academic and public, school library media centers and special—become full partners in a dynamic Learning Society. Given that happy change, the excellence of education in America can become a sound promise, rather than a forlorn dream.

[This report] stands as a framework on which the community itself must now build. In the long run, it will be up to dedicated artisans in national, state, and local positions to turn this framework into a new structure. Their ideas, their approaches, their strategies, blended in common effort, will construct a home to endure in the Information Age.

—From *Alliance for Excellence* (the librarians' response to *A Nation at Risk*, Department of Education, 1984)

THE LIBRARY OF THE FUTURE 1985

. . . The bottom line is that the world's libraries in the future will be increasingly digitized and globalized. Information from libraries will move instantaneously from one library to another and from libraries to businesses, government offices, and homes everywhere. The information will also be increasingly animated and sonic: Sound and motion will become a more important part of library materials—and perhaps records of smells, feels, and tastes will also become part of library collections.

Fragrances already are available on records that one can "play." A needle scratches the surface of the record, releasing the scents of the sea, a mountain top, or a flower garden. Such fragrances may eventually be stored in libraries, so that someone interested in flowers might be able to smell them while looking at pictures of them.

Tastes might also be recorded and would be a natural addition to cookbooks. It would be a tremendous advantage for a cook to be able to taste a dish before going to the labor of preparing it.

Recording the feel of objects without physically storing the objects themselves might seem a challenge, but they could be approximated, perhaps by the use of holographic techniques combined with robotics. An object would first be recorded in the form of digitized signals; later, it would be re-created, perhaps out of a plastic material that could be melted and reused.

The recording of objects such as statues, furniture, vases, etc., would make it possible for valued objects to be re-created if they were destroyed. Also, blind people could gain greater understanding of them.

Books or articles may increasingly be printed on demand at a library, as computers and laser printers make this procedure feasible. On-demand publishing could be one way to solve the storage problem that has become a real crisis for many libraries. You may be asked to pay for the book, but it would be yours to keep, with a small portion of your payment going to the book's author.

On-demand publishing would make it possible for many more books to be published than is the case now: An author would submit a single copy of his manuscript to an electronic publisher, who would then announce its availability to anyone interested along with the price for having a copy printed out. This procedure would greatly speed up the publication of books. A book could become available on the same day that an author completed a manuscript instead of having to wait for months while typesetters, printers, and distributors are pushing the book slowly through today's cumbersome publishing process.

Libraries that scorn information that is not in book form will play a declining role in the future, but libraries that embrace the newer technologies (without neglecting books, of course) should become increasingly valuable to their patrons.

Libraries enable the past to talk to the future. Here we can find the words of Plato and Jesus, Confucius and Franklin D. Roosevelt. In the future, libraries will do an even better job in handling this communication across space and time. The sights and sounds and even the tastes and smells of life today will be preserved in the libraries of the future for our children and grandchildren.

—From *The Futurist* (December 1985), by Edward Cornish, editor of the magazine

Nation of Readers As part of National Library Week in 1985, the ALA and the Center for the Book at the Library of Congress sponsored a photography contest based on the theme of "A Nation of Readers." More than 70,000 photos were submitted. These photos by Mark Roberts, William F. Thompson, and Susan Chase Novack are among 1200 winning images. (ALA)

BIBLIOGRAPHY

The following books and articles were of great help in preparing this book:

Ballard, Harlan H., *Adventures of a Librarian*, Walter Neale, New York, 1929.

Beniott, Bruce W., *The Library Book*, Minneapolis Public Library and Information Center, Minneapolis, 1984.

Brown, Eleanor Frances, *Bookmobiles and Bookmobile Service*, The Scarecrow Press, Metuchen, N.J., 1967.

Coutts, Henry T., *Library Jokes and Jottings*, Grafton and Co., London, 1914.

Cramer, C. H., *Open Shelves and Open Minds*, The Press of Case Western Reserve University, Cleveland, 1972.

Dain, Phyllis, *The New York Public Library*, The New York Public Library, New York, 1972.

Daniel, Hawthorne, *Public Libraries for Everyone*, Doubleday and Co., Garden City, N.Y., 1961.

Ditzion, Sidney, *Arsenals of a Democratic Culture*, American Library Association, Chicago, 1947.

Dunkin, Paul, *Tales of Melvil's Mouser or Much Ado About Libraries*, R. R. Bowker, New York, 1970.

Edwards, Margaret A., *The Fair Garden and the Swarm of Beasts*, Hawthorne Books, New York, 1969.

Ellsworth, Dianne J., and Norman D. Stevens, *Landmarks of Library Literature*, The Scarecrow Press, Metuchen, N.J., 1976.

Fairlie, Henry, "In Libraries, Worlds Overlap," *The Washington Post*, March 7, 1982.

Garrison, Dee, *Apostles of Culture*, The Free Press, New York, 1979.

Glover, Janice, *Lighter Side of the Library*, William S. Sullwold Publishing, Taunton, Mass., 1970.

Goodrum, Charles A., *The Library of Congress*, Praeger Publishers, New York, 1974.

Gulker, Virgil, *Books Behind Bars*, The Scarecrow Press, Metuchen, N.J., 1973.

Hall, Barbara B., *Folklore from Maine Libraries*, Unpublished report presented to the Northeast Folklore Archives, University of Maine, Orono, 1968.

Harris, Michael H., *Reader in American Library History*, Microcard Editions, Washington, D.C., 1971.

Holley, Edward G., Beta Phi Mu, Pittsburgh, 1967.

Kalish, Philip Arthur, *The Enoch Pratt Free Library: A Social History*, The Scarecrow Press, Metuchen, N.J., 1969.

Kaser, David, *A Book for Sixpence*, Beta Phi Mu, Pittsburgh, 1980.

Koch, Theodore Wesley, "Carnegie Libraries," *The Chautauquan Magazine*, June 1906.

Likins, John R., *From Adzes to Xerxes*, PLAFSEP Press, Wellesley Free Library, Wellesley, Mass., 1982.

Lord, Caroline M., *Diary of a Village Librarian*, New Hampshire Publishing Co., Somersworth, 1971.

MacLeish, Archibald, *Champion of a Cause*, American Library Association, Chicago, 1971.

McReynolds, Rosalee, "A Heritage Dismissed," *Library Journal*, November 1, 1985.

Marshall, John David, *An American Library History Reader*, Shoe String Press, Inc., Hamden, Conn., 1961.

———, *Books, Libraries, Librarians*, Shoe String Press, Hamden, Conn., 1955.

Munthe, Wilhelm, *American Librarianship from a European Angle*, American Library Association, Chicago, 1939.

Pawel, Ernst, "Terminal Libraries," *Newsday Magazine*, October 14, 1984.

Pearson, Edmund Lester, *The Librarian at Play*, Small, Maynard and Co., Boston, 1911.

Plotnik, Arthur, *Library Life—American Style*, The Scarecrow Press, Metuchen, N.J., 1975.

Ring, Daniel F., *Studies in Creative Partnership*, The Scarecrow Press, Metuchen, N.J., 1980.

Rose, Ernestine, *The Public Library in American Life*, Columbia University Press, New York, 1954.

Sass, Samuel, "Librarians vs. Authors," *Publisher's Weekly*, January 13, 1945.

Sayers, Frances Clarke, *Summoned by Books*, Viking Press, New York, 1965.

Schuchat, Theodor, *The Library Book*, Madrona Publishers, Seattle, 1985.

Shera, Jesse H., *Foundations of the Public Library*, University of Chicago Press, Chicago, 1949.

Vann, Sarah K., *Melvil Dewey: His Enduring Presence in Librarianship*, Libraries Unlimited, Littleton, Colo., 1978.

Wakin, Edward, "One for the Books," *American Way*, May 1983.

Wikander, Lawrence E., *Disposed to Learn: The First Seventy-Five Years of the Forbes Library*, Trustees of the Forbes Library, Northampton, Mass., 1972.

Woodford, Frank B., *Parnassus on Main Street*, Wayne State University Press, Detroit, 1965.

Young, Arthur P., *Books for Sammies*, Beta Phi Mu, Pittsburgh, 1981.

INDEX